Sewing with Letters

Sewing with Letters

Using your favourite words & fonts

Nicola Tedman & Sarah Skeate

Ivy Press

First published in the UK in 2014 by

Ivy Press
210 High Street
Lewes
East Sussex BN7 2NS
United Kingdom
www.ivypress.co.uk

British Library Cataloguing-in-Publication Data
A catalogue record for this book is available from
the British Library

ISBN: 978-1-78240-087-5

This book was conceived, designed and produced by
Ivy Press
Creative Director Peter Bridgewater
Publisher Susan Kelly
Conceived by Sophie Collins
Editorial Director Tom Kitch
Art Director James Lawrence
Designer Clare Barber
Photographer Neal Grundy
Illustrator Vicky Woodgate
Models Anna and William Stevens

Ivy Press would like to thank Dan Gneiding for
permission to use his font Ribbon and Peter Fritzsche
for permission to use his font Origami.

Printed in China

Colour origination by Ivy Press Reprographics

10 9 8 7 6 5 4 3 2 1

Distributed worldwide (except North America) by
Thames & Hudson Ltd, 181A High Holborn,
London WC1V 7QX, United Kingdom

Contents

Before You Start

The projects in this book include accessories you can make from scratch, as well as inspirational ideas for personalizing existing items. The designs vary in complexity so even if you're relatively inexperienced there will be plenty for you to make, but read this section before you start on your first project – you'll find it useful in helping you get the best possible finish.

FINDING FONTS

The fonts we've suggested you use are a mixture of those that may have come bundled with your computer's operating system and others that can be purchased online.

A few projects use specific words or phrases, and templates have been supplied for these. In other cases, you're free to choose your own initials or letters. Once you've established the font you want to use and loaded it on your computer, type the characters in the correct font in your word processing or desktop publishing programme, then simply change the font size to fit the project. Most programmes offer onscreen rulers or the option of viewing your work in a print layout view so you can scale your font's size accurately before printing it out. Instructions are provided for making templates or stencils to use in your chosen project.

EQUIPMENT

You'll only need basic crafting tools and sewing supplies for the majority of these projects, and all have full equipment as well as materials lists at the beginning, so that you can check that you have everything you'll need before you start. Some projects call for you to sew leather or suede, in which case a leather needle for your sewing machine will be necessary.

There are two other pieces of kit that are called for in a few projects and that may prove worth investing in: a laminator and a bias tape maker.

Laminator

A laminator is used to coat a piece of paper or card with flexible plastic. In these projects its use is sometimes suggested to help you to create hardy templates or stencils which can be used with paint. Laminators and the glue pouches that are used with them are invaluable to keen crafters, are relatively inexpensive and are easy to get hold of. If you decide you'd like one, check out the different models and sizes online to get the best deal; you'll find that there are plenty of options. It's worth investing in one of the bigger sizes, as this gives you the option of creating larger templates or stencils.

Bias tape maker

Bias tape makers are small and cheap, and can be found online or in the haberdashery departments in stores. You can buy them to create different widths of tape, but regular sewers may want to own several in different sizes—you simply pull your length of bias-cut fabric through a tape maker and it turns in the edges to create instant bias tape that you can then use for binding edges, making loops and so on. In this book, you'll find bias tape is also sometimes used to recreate flowing, calligraphic fonts.

TECHNIQUES
Sewing

The projects use both hand and machine sewing. Any special needles – ie for sewing leather or suede – are mentioned in the materials lists for the projects, which use a wide range of textiles and fabrics.

Hand sewing is generally straightforward. However, you may be unfamiliar with ladder stitch, which is used in a few of the projects. Ladder stitch is used to close gaps between two edges of fabric.

To sew ladder stitch, align the two fabric edges and bring the needle up from the wrong side of one piece of fabric, then stitch between the fabrics as shown in the diagram. Sew loosely, pulling the thread up to tighten it every few stitches.

If you are using fusible bonding web, simply hold the iron on the paper for a few seconds, then place it on another part – don't slide the iron around.

Gluing
FUSIBLE BONDING WEB

This is used to glue two fabrics together; the type used in this book has an adhesive and paper backing on one side. It is pressed directly onto the wrong side of the fabric you are using (the heat dissolves and activates the glue, so it fuses to the fabric).

INTERFACING

This is used to stiffen fabrics. The type used in this book has an iron-on adhesive on one side to allow it to be easily applied to fabrics.

GLUE

Two sorts of glue are specified in the projects. One is high-tack craft glue, which is very sticky. It's best to use it sparingly and to aim it accurately – a little goes a long way.

The second is contact glue, which has a strong hold provided it's used correctly. Spread a very thin layer of glue on both of the surfaces to be stuck together (a spatula spreader is useful here; some contact glue comes with one, ready to use), leave to dry for a minute or two, then press the surfaces firmly together to stick.

{Single-Letter} Tote Bag

There are so many appealing fonts easily available that it can be hard to pick the best for your project. For this very simple lettered bag, the letter that you choose must have a shadowed effect, so that you can use two contrasting colours of fabric. If you've only got an hour to spare, this project is a good choice – it's extremely easy and fast to do.

PERSONALIZING YOUR PROJECT

- Once you've mastered a single shadowed letter, try this simple technique for pairs of initials.
- You can also create inline letters by using thin cord sewn within the overall outline.

CHOOSING YOUR LETTER

Although any shadowed font will work for this project, try something simple if it's your first attempt. Below are some possible options.

YOU WILL NEED

Plain calico cotton tote bag

Two pieces of plain non-fraying lightweight cotton fabric, such as poplin, in complementary colours; the pieces need to be at least 31 x 25.5 cm (12 x 10 in.)

51 x 31 cm (20 x 12 in.) fusible bonding web

Sewing thread to match the fabrics

Sharp scissors

Non-permanent fabric pen

Metal ruler

Dressmaker's pins

DYNAMO SHADOW

GILL SANS SHADOWED

COMMERCE GOTHIC

BOKKA

PLEASURE BOLD SHADED

GILLIES GOTHIC

UMBRA

VICTORIAN INLINE

Although it calls for both an internal and an external show, Gill Sans Shadowed makes for an especially striking result.

Making the tote bag

1 Choose a font for the single letter that you want to use. For this project, you need a shadowed font, so pick one like the examples shown on page 9.

2 To make a template, print out the letter on plain paper, sized to fit one side of the tote bag. For most bags, you'll find that this means that the letter should be around 25.5 cm (10 in.) high.

3 Iron the tote bag. Cut the letter out of the paper and place it on the tote bag, positioning it centrally (use the ruler if you find it hard to do this by eye). When it's placed correctly, make some small marks around the edge with the non-permanent fabric pen so that you'll be able to position the final letter.

4 Cut up the letter so that you have separate pieces for the body and the shadow. This example has a single piece for the letter and three separate pieces for the shadow. Pin the letter pattern piece to one piece of fabric and the shadow pattern piece or pieces to the other. Draw around them with the non-permanent fabric pen.

2.

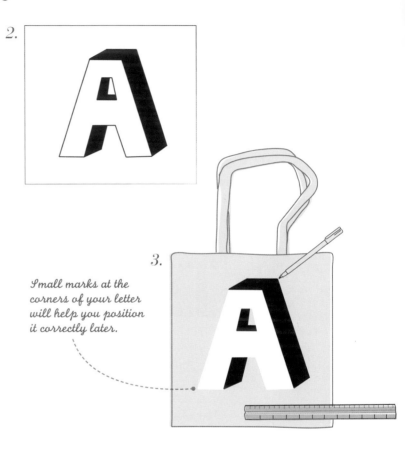

Small marks at the corners of your letter will help you position it correctly later.

3.

4.

5 Cut the fusible bonding web into two pieces, one for each piece of fabric. Apply the bonding web to the back of each piece of fabric. Cut the letter and shadow pieces out of the fabric.

6 Lay a clean, folded tea towel flat inside your tote bag, and place the bag on the ironing board, with the marked side facing upwards. Carefully peel the paper backing off the letter shape and lay it in place on the bag, then press with an iron until it is stuck to the bag. Repeat with the shadow pieces, being careful to align the shadow exactly with the letter.

7 For an especially hard-wearing finish, machine stitch around the edges of the letter, matching the thread to the fabric colours and using a small zigzag stitch.

5.

Check that your scissors are sharp enough to cut a clean line before you start.

6.

7.

The zigzag stitching needs to be very precise to look good, so practise on a scrap of fabric first.

Filled with blocks of soft foam and ornamented with a classic font – so they offer a first lesson in good design as well as letter recognition – these alphabet cubes are five times as pretty as anything you'll find in a shop. Although they take a little work to arrive at a crisp finished result, you can easily set up a production line to make a full alphabet: a dozen or more blocks are as simple to make as just one or two. Look out for fat-quarter bundles of suitable novelty prints, available from quilting shops and online.

PERSONALIZING YOUR PROJECT

- Instead of using one font with frames, try using a variety of different fonts without frames.
- Replace the novelty fabrics with simple felt outlines of objects stitched on to plain fabrics.

ABOUT THE FONT

Although it was inspired by the work of the Bauhaus designers in the mid-1920s to create an accessible, all-purpose font, the Bauhaus face was actually created in the mid-1970s by the American typographers Ed Benguiat and Victor Caruso.

The clean outlines of the Bauhaus font ensure that the letters are easy to cut from felt.

FOR EACH BLOCK YOU WILL NEED

Decorative frame on page 120

½ sheet A4-format inkjet T-shirt transfer paper for light fabrics

Two 13.5-cm (5¼-in.) squares of plain cotton

Two 7-cm (2¾-in.) squares of felt in contrasting colours

Two 13.5-cm (5¼-in.) squares of two different small-print cotton fabrics

Two 13.5-cm (5¼-in.) squares of natural textured linen or cotton

10-cm (4-in.) square of thin card to use as a template

Piece of upholstery foam, 10 cm (4 in.) thick

Stranded embroidery thread to match the felt colours

Sewing thread in a natural colour

Embroidery needle

Hi-tack craft glue

Craft knife

Sharp scissors

Pencil

Non-permanent fabric marker pen

Metal ruler

Dressmaker's pins

Making the blocks

1 Copy or scan the decorative frame for the blocks on page 120. Print the frame on to the T-shirt transfer paper, making as many copies as you need (you'll need two frames for each block), then cut out the frames.

2 Following the manufacturer's instructions, iron the T-shirt transfer paper on to the centre of each plain cotton square, leaving a 2-cm (¾-in.) gap around the edge of each frame for the border and the seam allowance.

3 Print out your chosen letters on to plain paper with the 'b' and 'd' 5.5 cm (2¼ in.) high. Cut them out neatly.

4 Pin each letter on to a piece of felt, draw around it using the non-permanent fabric marker pen and cut the characters out.

5 Position each felt letter carefully in the centre of one of the printed frames and stick it in place using hi-tack craft glue. Leave to dry.

6 Thread an embroidery needle with a single strand of thread to match the felt and hand stitch around the edge of each felt letter, using a small, neat overstitch.

1.

2.

4.

The pen outline will fade naturally after a few days.

7 In addition to the two squares with the frames and letters, for each block you will need one square each of the two small-print patterned fabrics and two squares of the natural textured plain linen or cotton. For each of the six pieces of fabric, take the 10-cm (4-in.) square card template, place it on the centre of the wrong side and draw around it with a pencil, adding a 1.5-cm (⅝-in.) seam allowance to each square.

8 Lay out the fabrics in the T-shape shown. Turn them right side down and pin the central strip of four squares together. If either of your patterned fabrics is directional, you will get the best result if you place the pattern the same way up as the letters.

9 Start to sew your cube together, taking 1.5-cm (⅝-in.) seam allowances throughout. Thread your sewing machine with natural-coloured thread. Alternating print and letter squares, starting with a print square, sew the two letter squares and the two print squares into a vertical strip, without stitching into the seam allowance. Make some additional stitches backwards and forwards at the beginning and end of each seam.

10 Stitch one natural linen or cotton square to each side of the top print square on the strip, to give a T-shape.

8.

10.

11 Working on the wrong side of the fabrics and pinning before you sew, stitch the next side of each of the linen squares to the sides of the closest letter square.

12 Repeat, sewing the next side of each of the linen squares to the second print square. When you've sewn all the seams, you will have an open fabric 'box' with a lid.

13 Stitch two of the three open sides of the fabric 'lid' down, so there is just one edge of the fabric cube open. Trim all the stitched seam allowances by half, then turn the cube right side out.

14 Cut a neat cube of upholstery foam 10 cm (4 in.) square, using a craft knife and metal ruler. Compressing it firmly with your fingers, push it into the fabric box, easing the box over the cube to fit it smoothly and get all the corners in place.

15 When the foam is neatly within the fabric, fold in the seam allowance of the open edge and pin it together. Thread the embroidery needle with natural-coloured sewing thread and neatly ladder stitch the seam closed.

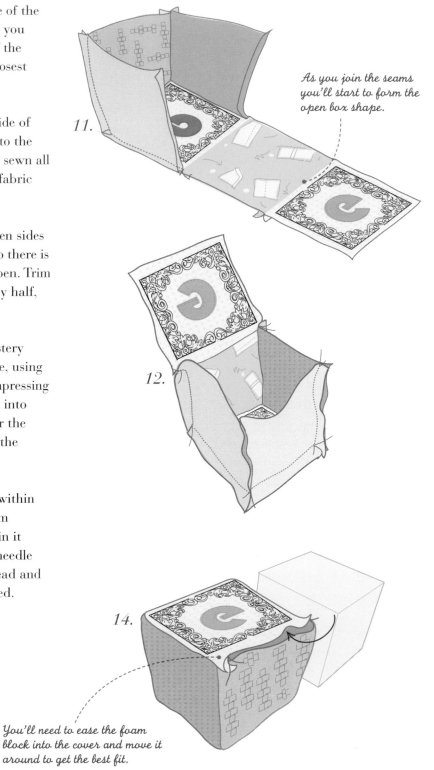

11.

As you join the seams you'll start to form the open box shape.

12.

14.

You'll need to ease the foam block into the cover and move it around to get the best fit.

{Tablet} Case

Thick, soft felt offers a degree of protection to your tablet computer – and, appliquéd with your initials, identifies it instantly as your property. It's worth tracking down this substantial felt weight, even if it isn't stocked in your local craft outlet; you can find it in various colours online. A dark or neutral colour sets off more vibrant initials in a lighter weight of felt – and a wrap-around, legal-style closure to match the initials adds the finishing touch. It's personal, protective and simple and economical to make.

PERSONALIZING YOUR PROJECT

- Century is a good choice for projects that call for single letters or pairs of initials, but the relatively bulky characters aren't so good for whole words.

ABOUT THE FONT
Century Regular

The original Century type was designed at the end of the nineteenth century by L.B. Benton, and was named for the periodical for which it was commissioned, *Century Magazine*. The commission specifically asked for a bold, legible font, with clean serifs and broad uprights and curves.

YOU WILL NEED

Template on page 125

61 x 25.5 cm (24 x 10 in.) felt, 5 mm (³/₁₆ in.) thick

20-cm (8-in.) square contrasting-coloured craft felt

Sheet of thin card (make sure it's suitable for use with your printer)

20-cm (8-in.) square fusible bonding web

51 cm (20 in.) waxed cotton cord, 2 mm (¹/₁₆ in.) in diameter

Two plastic buttons, 2 cm (¾ in.) in diameter, in colour to match craft felt

Top stitch thread to match thick felt

Sewing thread to match craft felt

Metal ruler

Craft knife

Sharp scissors

Cutting mat

Pencil

Non-permanent fabric marker pen or tailor's chalk

Cloth tape measure

Dressmaker's pins

The large serifs demand you leave ample space between your letters if you use more than one.

Making the case

1 Use the tape measure to measure all around the tablet you're making the case for. Take the exact measurements of both the length and the width.

2 Halve the width measurement and add 12 mm (½ in.) for the seam allowances. Using the craft knife and metal ruler on a cutting mat, cut the thick felt strip to this width.

3 Use the tape measure to transfer the complete length measurement – around both the front and back of the long side of the tablet as well as the ends – to the felt strip, and mark the top end with pins.

4 Copy or scan the template on page 125, enlarging it to match the width of your felt strip, then print and cut it out. Pin it to the felt, immediately above the line of pins that you used to mark the top of the case.

5 Cut around the curve of the flap neatly with sharp scissors.

1.

Measure carefully – the accuracy of these dimensions determines the fit of your case.

2.

4.

Align the straight edge of the flap exactly with the pin markers.

6 Bring the lower edge of the strip up to meet the pins at the base of the flap. Press the fold at the base of the cover firmly with your fingers and mark it with pins, then unfold the strip.

7 Print out on to thin card the letters you have chosen at a size where they are 4 cm (1½ in.) narrower than the width of the felt strip. Using a craft knife on a cutting mat, cut the letters out, leaving small strips to hold the centres of the letters in place if necessary.

8 Following the manufacturer's instructions, apply fusible bonding web to the wrong side of the craft felt.

9 Reverse the card stencil, draw your letters on the paper backing of the fusible bonding web with a pencil, and cut them out.

10 Peel the backing paper off the fusible bonding web. Using the stencil to check that they're level and the right distance apart, position the letters on the front of the case, 2 cm (¾ in.) above the fold at the base.

11 Lay a clean tea towel over the letters and the thick felt strip and press the letters into position, using a hot iron.

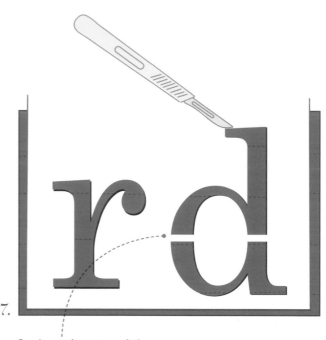

7.

Don't cut the strips of the stencil too finely or you risk them breaking.

10.

12 Thread your sewing machine with thread to match the craft felt and topstitch a neat line just inside the edge of the felt letters. (Turning the machine wheel by hand will give you more control when working around tight curves.)

13 Fold the case along the fold at the base, right side out, and pin down the side seams. Thread your sewing machine with the thread to match the thick felt and, starting from one bottom corner, topstitch all the way around the sides and the top of the flap, 5 mm (³⁄₁₆ in.) in from the outside edge. Make some additional stitches forwards and backwards when you begin and end your stitching. Leave the fold at the bottom of the case unstitched.

14 Fold the flap over and make a mark on the front of the flap, centred on the width of the case. Using the topstitching thread, sew one of the buttons on at this point, just above the topstitching line. Then stitch the second button to the front of the case, positioning it so that it lies immediately below the first button when the flap is folded down.

15 Cut a 36-cm (14-in.) length of the waxed cord and tie a knot close to either end. Knot the cord around the top button on the case, about 6 cm (2½ in.) in from one end. Wrap the cord around the buttons in a figure-of-eight shape to hold the case shut.

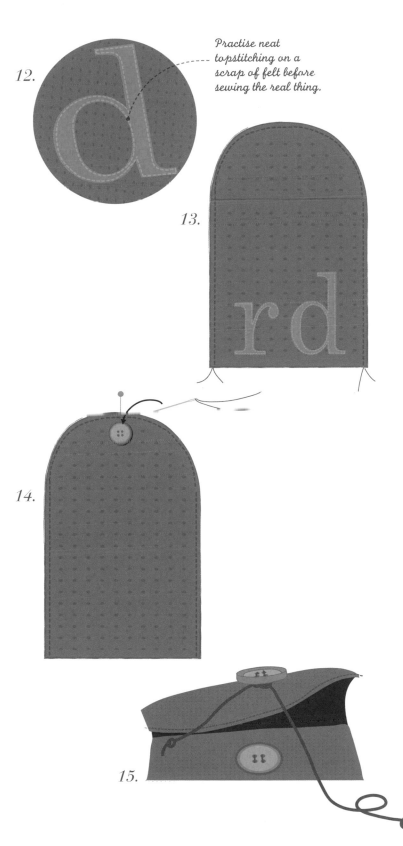

12.

Practise neat topstitching on a scrap of felt before sewing the real thing.

13.

14.

15.

{Lettered} Cushions

These cushions, with their gently shaded 'OH', make a soft exclamation on your sofa. You could add some punctuation on a third cushion (a question mark? An exclamation mark?) if you want them to have more emphasis. The examples in the photo are made from raw silk, which has a slightly 'shot' look in strong light; felt would also work well, and you could use bright or even neon colours to give more of a Pop-Art effect. The covers are made to an envelope pattern, so that it's easy to slip a cushion pad inside.

PERSONALIZING YOUR PROJECT

- Try a set of cushions in the same or toning fabrics but using letters from a variety of fonts.
- Eurostile's square characters are best used quite large on items such as towels or cushions.

ABOUT THE FONT
EUROSTILE BOLD

Developed at the Nebiolo type foundry in Turin in 1962, Eurostile was an extension of an earlier, popular font, Microgramma.

Developed when much type design was deliberately 'modern' in feel, Eurostile's square capitals with their slightly rounded corners looked typically fresh and slightly futuristic.

FOR TWO CUSHIONS YOU WILL NEED

Templates on page 122
91 x 31-cm (36 x 12-in.) piece of fusible bonding web
Two 31-cm (12-in.) squares of grey felt
31-cm (12-in.) square of cream felt
46-cm (18-in.) square sheet of brown paper
51 cm (20 in.) each of two colours of raw silk (we used dusty pink and pale green), 115 cm (45 in.) wide
Two 46-cm (18-in.) square cushion pads
Sewing thread in grey, cream, pink and green
Sharp scissors
Pencil
Compass
Chalk pencil or tailor's chalk
Metal ruler
Dressmaker's pins

Making the cushions

1 Copy or scan the templates on page 122, enlarging them to scale, then print and cut them out.

2 Cut the shadows away from the letters, so that you have three pieces for the 'O' (one letter piece and two shadows) and four pieces for the 'H' (one letter piece and three shadows).

3 Cut the fusible bonding web into three 31-cm (12-in.) squares. Following the manufacturer's instructions, apply one piece to the back of each of the three felt squares.

4 Place the main letter templates, reversed, on the bonding-web side of the grey felt squares, one letter on each of the squares. Draw around the templates and cut the letter shapes out.

5 Place all the shadow templates, reversed, on the bonding-web side of the cream felt square. Draw around the templates and cut the shadow shapes out.

Align the shadow pieces against the main letter pieces as you cut to ensure an accurate fit.

2.

4.

5.

6 Fold the brown paper square diagonally in both directions and crease sharply, then unfold, so that there is a fold line leading to each corner.

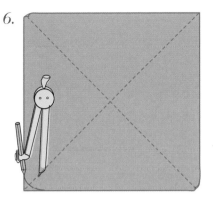

6.

7 Use the ruler to set the compasses to 7.5 cm (3 in.) and place the point about 11 cm (4¼ in.) up the fold line away from the corner, then draw a rounded corner. Repeat on the other three corners and cut the paper so that you have a square shape with rounded corners.

8 Fold the pattern in half vertically and horizontally and crease sharply, then unfold.

9 To make the pink 'O' cushion, take the pink silk and mark a central horizontal line and a central vertical one on it with a chalk pencil lightly on the right side of the fabric.

9.

The chalk marks will help you to size the cover correctly after the letter is appliquéd on to the front.

10 Peel off the backing paper from the grey felt 'O' piece and position it centrally on the front of the pink silk, using a ruler and the chalk lines to make sure that it's accurately placed. Cover with a clean tea towel and press with a warm iron.

11 Peel off the backing paper from the two cream felt shadow pieces and put them in place alongside the letter. Cover with a clean tea towel and press with a warm iron.

10.

12 Thread the sewing machine with grey thread and zigzag stitch around the inside and outside edges of the 'O'. Rethread the machine with cream thread and zigzag stitch around the inside and outside edges of the cream shadow pieces.

13 Lay the fabric face down on your work surface and add horizontal and vertical lines with a chalk pencil as you did in step 9. Place the brown-paper pattern on top of it, aligning the horizontal and vertical folds with the chalk lines.

14 Draw around the paper pattern with a chalk pencil. This will ensure that the letter is in the centre of the cushion.

15 Fold the selvedges at the sides of the fabric underneath once to the wrong side. Thread the sewing machine with pink thread and stitch the edges down.

16 Lay the fabric right side up on your work surface and fold the left-hand side of the fabric over to the centre, folding it along the chalk-marked pattern edge.

12.

Place the pattern exactly centrally using the chalk lines you drew earlier.

14.

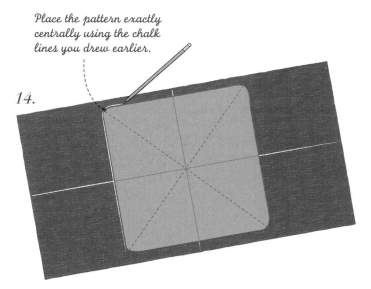

15.

The selvedge turns will form the edges of the envelope closure of the cushion.

17 Repeat with the right-hand side of the fabric so that the edge overlaps the left-hand edge. Pin around the open edges of the fabric, going through all the layers.

18 Turn the cover over, so that you can see the chalk outline of the cushion pattern. Using matching thread in the machine, sew the cover closed along the top and bottom, going around the curves on the corners. There is no need to stitch the straight sides, as these are on the folds of the fabric.

19 Trim the seam allowances along the top and bottom to 1 cm (⅜ in.). Zigzag stitch around the raw edges of the seam allowances. Turn the cushion cover right way out and press, then insert a cushion pad.

20 To make the second cover, repeat steps 9–19, using the felt and fabric for the 'H' cushion.

17.

18.

19.

Zigzag-stitched edges will ensure the fabric does not fray.

{Monogrammed} Dog Jumper

Your beloved pet deserves the best – and his own initial on his own jacket (in, perhaps, your or his favourite font) reflects that. This is simply worked as an appliqué patch that can be neatly stitched to any dog coat. Our instructions are for a medium-sized patch, but if your pet weighs in at either end of the size spectrum (huge or tiny), you can scale the size of the circle and letter up or down to suit.

PERSONALIZING YOUR PROJECT

- Cooper Black doesn't have any fine points or thin strokes, so it can be adapted to any project that uses stencils and fabric paint.
- You could try overlapping letters in different colours for a different look.

ABOUT THE FONT

Designed in the 1920s by Oswald Bruce Cooper of Chicago, Cooper Black has hefty outlines combined with relatively modest serifs – a classic display face. It was originally advertised as being for 'far-sighted printers with near-sighted customers'.

YOU WILL NEED

Dog coat or jumper with a plain back

15-cm (6-in.) square of fusible bonding web

15-cm (6-in.) square of red fleece fabric

25.5-cm (10-in.) square of cream flannel sheeting

25.5-cm (10-in.) square of heat-resistant wadding

19-cm (7½-in.) diameter circle of thin card

Red and cream sewing threads

Embroidery needle

Pencil

Non-permanent fabric marker pen

Sharp scissors

Dressmaker's pins

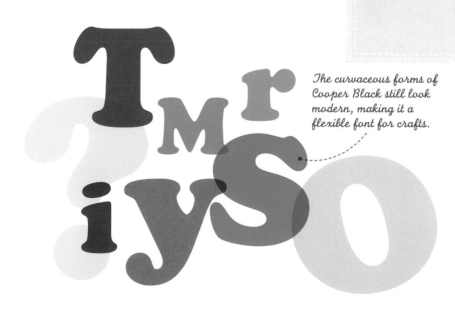

The curvaceous forms of Cooper Black still look modern, making it a flexible font for crafts.

Making the dog jumper

1 Print out your chosen letter at a size where it is no taller or wider than 12 cm (4¾ in.) and cut it out.

2 Following the manufacturer's instructions, press the fusible bonding web on to the wrong side of the fleece fabric with an iron.

3 Reverse your letter template and lay it on the wrong side of the fleece. Pin it in place and draw around it with a pencil, then remove the pins and carefully cut it out.

4 Turn the letter right side up. Peel off the backing paper from the bonding web and iron the fleece letter on to the centre of the piece of flannel sheeting, placing it on the diagonal.

5 Place the flannel sheeting on top of the wadding, align the edges and pin the layers together. Thread the sewing machine with red thread and work carefully around the edge of the letter, using a wide satin stitch. You may find it easier to turn the wheel by hand to keep control of the stitching around the details of the letter.

1.

3.

5.

Pin the layers together thoroughly so they don't shift about as you machine around your initial.

6. Turn the flannel square face down and carefully position the thin card circle over the letter, making sure the letter is centred in the circle. Draw around the circle on to the wadding with a fabric marker.

7. Carefully cut around the drawn circle, cutting out the wadding layer only.

8. Draw a line around the edge of the cut-out circle, 1.5 cm (⅝ in.) beyond the edge, and cut around the flannel layer.

9. Thread an embroidery needle with a double strand of cream thread and work a small running stitch by hand 6 mm (¼ in.) in from the raw edge of the flannel. When you've sewn all the way around, pull the threads to gather the edge of the flannel, so that the gathered edge lies on the back of the patch. Knot the thread.

10. Thread a needle with a single strand of cream thread and hand stitch the edge of the flannel down to the back of the wadding near the edge to keep your patch flat, taking care not to stitch through to the front of the patch.

11. Pin the patch right way up to the centre back of the dog coat. Using cream thread and a small ladder stitch, sew the patch on to the coat.

Draw the thread up slowly and evenly to gather the circle around the initial.

This stylish washbag made from waterproof fabric uses red and blue on white for a crisp colour combination. This clean design features a stylized showerhead plus the Spanish word for 'bath', but you can use a different word or language. However, it's best to use a short word because the smaller the letters get, the more fiddly they will be to cut out neatly. We've suggested that you use a laminating machine to make the pattern – they're inexpensive and help you get an ultra-neat finish – but you can make the bag without one, using thin card to make the stencil instead.

PERSONALIZING YOUR PROJECT

- You could make a set, with a different-coloured bag for each member of the family.
- You can experiment with heavier waterproof fabrics for larger, outdoor projects.

ABOUT THE FONT
FUTURA MEDIUM

Balanced and functional, Futura is the best-known face designed by Paul Renner, a German typographer. He intended it to be workable across a wide range of applications and it is still a popular choice for everything from signage to book design.

YOU WILL NEED

Pattern on page 122

Laminating machine and glued laminating pouch (or you can print or trace the pattern on to thin card)

23 x 7.5 cm (9 x 3 in.) red leatherette fabric

13 x 13 cm (5 x 5 in.) blue leatherette fabric

61 x 31 cm (24 x 12 in.) waterproof nursery sheeting; this has a rubber coating on one side and a woven fabric on the other

31-cm (12-in.) white zip with a closed end

Blue, red and white sewing thread

Craft knife

Sharp scissors

Cutting mat

Ballpoint pen

Pencil

Hi-tack craft glue

Metal ruler

Dressmaker's pins

m f g *
W i b o

Futura is a moderate face, based on symmetry.

Making the washbag

1 Copy or scan the template on page 122, enlarging it to scale, then print and cut it out. Either copy it on to thin card to use as a template or put your paper through a laminating machine in a glued pouch.

2 Cut out the showerhead, the water drops and the lettering, leaving some small strips connecting the central sections of the 'B', the 'A' and the 'O', so that the centres stay in place.

3 Turn the stencil over (so the letters read in reverse), and use a ballpoint pen to mark out the letters on the back of the red leatherette. Cut the letters out carefully using a craft knife and a metal ruler on a cutting mat.

4 Repeat the process with the showerhead and water drops pattern, using the blue leatherette.

Tape the leatherette to a cutting board if it helps — it makes it easier to cut the letters out.

5 Lay out the rectangle of nursery sheeting and mark the middle of the upper 31-cm (12-in.) edge with a pencil. Place the stencil on the sheeting, centring it so that the top of the showerhead is aligned with the edge of the fabric and is in the middle of the strip. Use a pencil to mark some points at the corners and along the edges of the letters, the showerhead shape and the water drops.

6 Remove the stencil and use hi-tack craft glue to stick the leatherette pieces in place, using the guide marks you have made. Leave to dry. (If you put the fabric under a pile of glossy magazines, it will help the letters stick evenly to get the best result.)

7 Thread your sewing machine with blue thread and stitch neatly just inside the edges of the showerhead pattern and the drops. Rethread the machine with red thread and repeat, this time stitching inside the edges of the letters.

5.

6.

Use the glue sparingly; you don't need much.

7.

It may be easier to turn the wheel of the machine by hand when you are outlining small areas.

8 Pin the zip along the top edge of the rectangle, with the right side of the zip facing the right side of the fabric. Thread the sewing machine with white thread and stitch a line through zip and fabric, 6 mm (¼ in.) down from the top edge, reverse stitching for 2.5 cm (1 in.) at the start and the finish.

9 Fold the fabric over, right sides together, and pin the other side of the zip along the opposite short edge of the fabric. Stitch again. You will now have a tube of fabric, joined by the zip.

10 Turn the bag right side out and undo the zip. Fold the fabric back down away from the zip edge. Pin the fabric down and stitch along both sides of the zip again.

8.

Practise machining on a scrap of waterproof fabric to get the tension even before you sew the zip in place.

9.

10.

11 Close the zip again and turn the bag inside out, keeping the zip pull inside the bag. Pin the open sides together, folding the bag so that the zip falls 2.5 cm (1 in.) down from the top edge. Using white thread, stitch down both sides of the bag, 6 mm (¼ in.) in from the edges of the fabric, stitching over the zip and reverse stitching at the start and finish.

12 Trim off the excess zip tape flush with the fabric edge, and use a small line of zigzag machine stitch to stop it fraying.

13 To make the lower corners and give the washbag a flat base, flatten out a lower corner of one of the seamed sides of the bag, as shown, so that the seam is on top of the fold. Pin it flat, then take a ruler and mark with a pencil a line 6 cm (2½ in.) long at 90 degrees to the seam.

14 Stitch along the line, reverse stitching at the start and finish, then cut off the corner 6 mm (¼ in.) below the stitching. Repeat steps 13 and 14 with the second corner, then turn the bag right side out.

Flatten the corner of the washbag thoroughly before marking the line across it.

M ade from hard-wearing canvas, weighted with dried beans and adorned with a single bold and cheerful two-tone letter, this doorstop would make a terrific house-warming gift. It's quick to make, and the two-colour treatment of a single letter ensures that it makes a strong visual impact. The template is for a letter that narrows at the top slightly – you will need to adjust it if the letter you choose to use is a significantly different shape, such as a 'W' which will require a wider, squarer shape.

PERSONALIZING YOUR PROJECT

- Dividing single letters into coloured halves can work well with any font, provided that the font is both bold and simple enough to take it.

ABOUT THE FONT
BERNARD MT CONDENSED

Bold and chunky, Bernard looks as though it might be a product of the 1960s, so it's a surprise to learn that it was first issued commercially in 1926. You can see its origins in some of the blocky advertising fonts of the late nineteenth century: it's readable, but still has plenty of personality.

a g e k
o r

Lower-case characters in Bernard have some surprisingly narrow strokes, so they're a little more challenging to cut neatly.

YOU WILL NEED

Templates on pages 120–1

1-m (1-yd) length mid-weight cream canvas fabric

31-cm (12-in.) square turquoise felt

31-cm (12-in.) square dark blue felt

31-cm (12-in.) square fusible bonding web

31 cm (12 in.) striped or checked ribbon, 2.5 cm (1 in.) wide

Bag polyester toy filling

1 kg (2 lb 4 oz) dried rice

Tacking thread

Cream sewing thread

Sewing needle

Sharp scissors

Non-permanent fabric marker pen

Pencil

Hi-tack craft glue

Metal ruler

Dressmaker's pins

Making the doorstop

1 Print out your chosen letter 23 cm (9 in.) high. Select the appropriate pattern pieces on pages 120–1 for the size and shape of your letter, then copy or scan them, enlarge to scale and print them out.

2 Cut roughly around the paper template (at this stage you don't need to cut out any internal space such as centre of the 'A'). Using a ruler, draw a pencil line across the back of the template exactly halfway up the letter.

3 Next, cut out the pattern pieces to make the body of the doorstop and pin them on to the canvas. Cut around them, leaving a 2.5-cm (1-in.) seam allowance around each piece.

2.

Make sure that your horizontal line is exactly level, so that your finished letter will look balanced.

3.

Make sure you leave a 2.5-cm (1-in.) seam allowance around each template.

4 Lay out your two felt pieces, aligning them together along a horizontal axis. Place the fusible bonding web on top of them, with the bonding agent facing down and the peel-off backing facing up. Finally put the letter template wrong side up on top, precisely aligning the centre pencil line along the line where the two colours of felt meet. Use tiny dots of hi-tack craft glue in the corners of the paper template to hold it in place on top of the bonding web.

5 Cover with a clean tea towel and press with a warm iron.

6 Now carefully cut the letter out of the felt using scissors.

7 Lay the letter right side up on the front canvas panel of your doorstop. Use a ruler to place it centrally, then make small marks around the edges of the letter with a non-permanent fabric marker pen, so that you can re-position it accurately. Peel off the backing paper from the bonding web and carefully position the letter on the canvas following your marks. Place a clean cloth over the felt, then press in place with a medium-hot iron.

The pencil guides will ensure you place the letters accurately.

8 With the wrong sides facing out, pin and tack the short sides of the base and side pieces of your doorstop together, then thread your sewing machine with the cream thread and sew the three pieces into a strip, taking a 2.5-cm (1-in.) seam allowance. Press the seams open. Pin and tack the front and back pieces in place, easing the sides into place to fit, so that you have an open-topped bag, then machine stitch, again taking a 2.5-cm (1-in.) seam allowance. Press the seams open and trim the corners.

9 Pin the ribbon to the sides of the top piece of the doorstop, then tack the top in place along both sides and the front, leaving the back top edge open. Machine stitch the seams, then turn the doorstop right side out.

10 Pad the base of the doorstop with a thin layer of polyester toy filling to a depth of about 5 cm (2 in.), then pour in the rice to weight the doorstop. When all the rice has been added, shake the doorstop so that it's weighted evenly, then add pieces of toy stuffing until the whole doorstop is firmly padded.

11 Turn under the raw edges of the last open seam, thread a sewing needle with cream thread and slipstitch the gap closed.

Trimming the corners where the seams meet will give your doorstep sharper corners when it's turned right way out.

{Café} Blind

Old-fashioned café blinds were originally designed to provide a little privacy behind a window opening out on to the street, but without blocking out light. Our version is made from light linen and muslin, so the blind, hung from an elastic from the halfway point on the window, remains translucent. Our blind is about one metre square; you may need to adjust the sizes of the muslin and linen depending on the size of your window.

PERSONALIZING YOUR PROJECT

- Calligraphic fonts make for gorgeous results, but take your time planning their use – they call for a sharp and immaculate finish.

ABOUT THE FONT

Bickham Script

Inspired by an eighteenth-century manual, *The Universal Penman*, and named for its author, George Bickham, this font was in fact created in the late 1990s by the American typographer Richard Lipton. Beautiful and showy, it's best used in small doses.

Lovely, but challenging: the lavish curlicues of Bickham call for a steady hand as you work.

YOU WILL NEED

Template on page 125

Two 121 x 25.5-cm (48 x 10-in.) strips natural muslin fabric

121 x 63 cm (48 x 25 in.) beige linen fabric

Two sheets A4-format T-shirt transfer paper for light fabrics

Sewing thread in natural colour

Darning needle

Pencil

Masking tape

1-m (1-yd) metal ruler

Dressmaker's pins

Making the blind

1 Lay the muslin strips on top of either side of the long edges of the linen, then pin them together. Thread the sewing machine with the natural-coloured thread and sew the strips on either side of the linen, taking a 12-mm (½-in.) seam.

2 Press the two seams flat with a hot iron, pressing them towards the muslin edges of the blind.

3 Machine a second line of stitching 6 mm (¼ in.) into the seam allowance, along the pressed edges of the fabric.

4 Use the darning needle to pull out some threads along the raw edge of the fabric on the seam allowances to create a delicately frayed edge (the second row of stitching will prevent the fabric from fraying too far).

1.

Pull out the edge threads one at a time — it's easier than trying to remove several in one go.

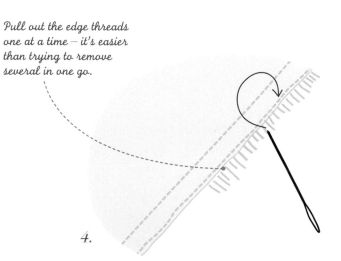

4.

5 Now hem the sides of the blind: use the ruler and a pencil to mark a line 5 cm (2 in.) in from the long raw edges of the muslin, fold the raw edges up to the pencil lines and press, then fold the edges again and press to create a 2.5 cm (1 in.) hem. Machine stitch along the hems on both sides of the blind.

6 Spread out your blind and, if necessary, trim the top edge to a straight line (muslin is a very open fabric and can stretch a little as you work). Create a hem aross the top edge, folding and pressing as in the previous step.

7 Pin in place, then machine stitch a line of stitching close to the bottom edge of the turned top of the blind, securing with a few reverse stitches at the beginning and end of the seam. You now have an open channel at the top of the blind to hold the curtain wire.

8 Repeat steps 5 and 6 to create a hem at the bottom edge of the blind. As the lower hem does not need to form a channel, stitch along the opening at either end of it to make a neat finish.

7.

8.

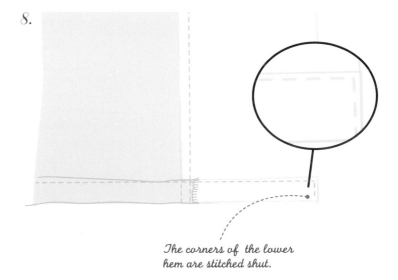

The corners of the lower hem are stitched shut.

9 Copy or scan the template for 'Café' from page 125 and enlarge to scale. Following the manufacturer's instructions, print the word on to the transfer paper (remember, the word is reversed in order to appear the right way round on the blind). Depending on the size of the paper you are using, you may need to split the template into multiple sections before printing and rejoin them after printing them out.

10 Cut the lettering out, leaving about 2 to 3 mm (¹⁄₁₆ to ⅛ in.) around the edges – particularly around the narrowest parts of the characters. Butt the pieces of the word together and join them with strips of masking tape, cutting away any excess tape when the parts are joined.

11 Carefully position the lettering in the centre of the linen strip on your blind, and use the ruler to check it is straight.

12 Iron the word in place, following the manufacturer's instructions, then carefully peel the backing off the transfer paper and hang your blind.

10.

11.

12.

As the transfer backing is peeled off, the coloured lettering is revealed.

{Folded-Letter} Table Linen

Fonts that play visual tricks are best used sparingly in fabric projects: after all, you still want to be able to make the letters out. These napkins, made with a simple stencilling technique, show off the elaborate 'folds' of a modern alphabet which deliberately mimics origami forms.

PERSONALIZING YOUR PROJECT

- Novelty fonts which copy natural forms – from butterflies to bubbles and folded paper to woodgrain – can be charming but still practical enough to use.

ABOUT THE FONT

A contemporary font created by the German designer Peter Fritzsche, Origami was originally based on folded strips of paper and looks convincingly three-dimensional. It's best used for initals rather than phrases, allowing you to enjoy its ingenious forms.

YOU WILL NEED

White cotton napkins

A4 sheets of white paper

Laminator and glued laminating pouches

Two 31-cm (12-in.) squares of corrugated card

Craft knife

Ballpoint pen

Five fine-tipped fabric painting pens in fluorescent colours (you can buy these in packs)

Metal ruler

Dressmaker's pins

With a font as structurally complex as this one, you may prefer to stick to a single colour to keep the characters clear-cut.

Making the table linen

1 Print out your chosen sets of initials (or single letters) 5 cm (2 in.) high. You'll be able to get several sets on a single sheet of paper. Leave a margin of 2.5 cm (1 in.) from the edge of the paper and 5 cm (2 in.) between each pair of letters.

2 Laminate the paper using a laminator and a glued laminating pouch. Cut each set of initials into a separate rectangle, leaving a margin of at least 2.5 cm (1 in.) around the edges. Then, using the craft knife and ruler, cut each set of initials out to make the stencils.

3 Iron the napkins. Measure the depth of the hem on the napkins.

4 On each stencil, measure the hem's depth plus 2 mm (1/16 in.) down from the base of the letters. Draw a horizontal line parallel to the base of the letters at this point and cut off any excess to make the baseline of your stencil.

5 Measure from the outer edges of the letters on each of the stencils to find the centre point and mark it with a ballpoint pen.

1.

2.

Be careful not to break the narrow links between the letter pieces as you cut.

5.

The centre point is halfway between the overall width of both the letters and the space between them.

6 Fold your napkins in half and mark the centre point of one edge with a pin, then unfold your napkins.

7 Lay a double layer of corrugated card on your work surface and add a couple of layers of plain white paper on top. Lay a napkin on top of the stack.

8 Line up the centre marks on the stencil and napkin and use pins to fix the stencil in place. If you splay the pins outwards from the letter spaces, you will find it easier to colour the letters in.

9 Take a fine-nibbed fabric pen and draw around the outline of each letter. Use the pen with a light touch – if you stop too long in the corners of the stencil, the ink from the pen will bleed into the fabric and the sharp corners of the letters will be lost. After completing the outlines, colour the letters in using straight, even strokes.

10 Set the fabric ink with an iron, following the manufacturer's instructions. Repeat all the steps for each napkin, using a different fluorescent colour for the initials on each one.

6.

8.

9.

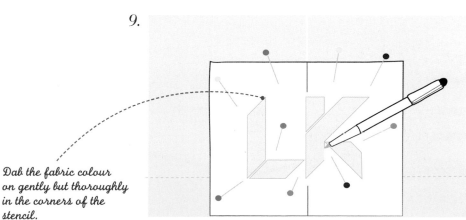

Dab the fabric colour on gently but thoroughly in the corners of the stencil.

{Ampersand} Bookends

You can make matching ampersands for a pair of these bookends or use different letters – the only limit is that, to be functional, the characters you choose must have some weight at the base to balance the weight of the books. Arial is a practical, balanced font, so will work well here, as would other even sans-serif shapes such as Gill Sans or Helvetica. The extra-thick felt can be found online if it isn't available in your local craft store.

PERSONALIZING YOUR PROJECT

- The thick felt cuts to make good sturdy font shapes, so you could experiment with larger letters to make items such as a child's play mat or a hanging storage pocket.

ABOUT THE FONT

Arial Bold

A modern font, first released to the market in 1982 by Monotype Typography, Arial has been described by one of the team who designed it, Robin Nicholas, as 'a generic sans serif'. Its outlines are neat and practical, and its slightly generic quality makes it endlessly flexible.

FOR EACH BOOKEND YOU WILL NEED

Template on page 121

80 x 25 cm (31½ x 9¾ in.) grey felt, 5 mm (³⁄₁₆ in.) thick

2 m (2 yd) waxed cotton cord, 2 mm (³⁄₁₆ in.) in diameter (found online or in craft stores); we used pink

1 kg (2 lb 4 oz) dry lentils or small plastic toy-filling pellets

Small quantity of toy stuffing

Craft knife

Sharp scissors

Cutting mat

Hole punch

Black fine-tipped felt pen

Latex contact adhesive

Craft glue

Glue spreader or small craft spatula

Metal ruler

Funnel or pouring jug

Dressmaker's pins

Uppercase letters will work best for this project – 'G', 'C', 'B', 'D' or 'U' would all be good picks.

Making the bookends

1 Copy or scan the template on page 121, enlarging it to scale, then print and cut it out. Use the smallest setting on the hole punch to punch the holes shown on the pattern.

2 Place the pattern on the grey felt and cut out the two sides of the ampersand. Position the pattern as economically as possible, as the strips to make the edges of the ampersand are cut from the remainder of the felt.

3 On the right side of one of the felt ampersands, mark all the holes through the pattern with the fine-tipped pen and, using the smallest setting on the hole punch, punch them through. Leave the other side unmarked.

4 Using a metal ruler and a craft knife on a cutting mat, cut the remainder of the felt into strips 5 cm (2 in.) wide. Make sure that you keep the strips as long as possible – you will need at least one that is a minimum of 37 cm (14½ in.) long, so that you can use it to make the top of the ampersand with no joins.

1.

3.

4.

Arrange the felt so that you can cut as many long strips from the leftovers as possible.

5 To make the inner edges of the ampersand, start with the internal holes. Place the front (pierced) side wrong side up on a solid work surface and stand one of the 5-cm (2-in.) strips on its edge. Starting at the corner of the upper hole, curve the strip around the hole. Push pins through both pieces at an angle to hold the strip in place, pinning it around the hole, flush with the edge of the felt. Where the strip crosses back on itself at the base of the hole, make a mark with the fine-tipped pen to show where the short end of the felt touches the inside surface of the strip.

6 Unpin the strip and cut it across at an exact right angle at the pen mark.

7 Use the glue spreader or spatula to scrape a 5-mm (³⁄₁₆-in.) wide line of latex contact adhesive around the hole, going right to the edges. Then spread a very thin layer of glue along one of the long edges of the strip.

8 Leave the glue to dry completely, or speed it up with a hairdryer. The glue should have gone completely transparent before you stick it (it's opaque when still damp).

5.

Hold the strip at exact right angles to the front piece as you pin it in place.

6.

The layer of glue on both pieces should be spread very thin.

7.

9 Position the strip around the hole on the front piece. Pinch along the seam really hard between your thumb and first two fingers to make sure it sticks securely.

10 Spread a very thin layer on one end of the felt strip across the thickness of the felt itself and another thin layer on the inner edge of the other end. Leave to dry as before and, when opaque, pinch the edges together firmly along the join.

11 Repeat the process with another strip of felt around the second hole in the front piece.

12 Now stick strips around the outside of the ampersand front, using the same technique. The diagram shows you how the strips should fit together. Use the longest strip around the top of the ampersand front, so that your finished bookend will have a smooth top, without joins.

13 Thread the pink cord through the pre-punched holes in the front in a running-stitch pattern, using one piece around each of the internal holes and one piece around the outer edge. At the end of each stitching round, tie the two cord ends together, cut the ends to 2 cm (¾ in.) and use craft glue on the ends to ensure that they won't come undone.

10.

Look at the circled joins of the felt strips on the right and follow them to make the sides of the ampersand.

12.

13.

14 Place the ampersand face down on your work surface. Mark a gap at the top with pins, to ensure that you leave a gap for the filling as you glue the shape together.

14.

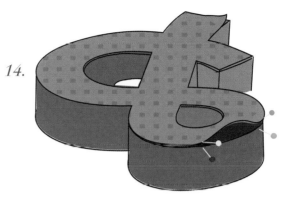

15 As before, scrape a very fine line of latex contact adhesive around the edge of the back piece and along the edges of the strips that form the gusset of the ampersand. Leave to dry, then position the back piece over the glued edges and pinch firmly all along the ampersand's outer edge to secure.

15.

16 Using a funnel or pouring jug, fill the ampersand through the gap at the top with the lentils or plastic toy pellets. Fill the shape roughly up to the halfway point, where the upper and lower loops meet. Fill the balance with toy stuffing, pushing small quantities into the gap until the ampersand is solidly filled.

17 Glue along the sides of the gap using latex contact adhesive. Leave to dry, then align the sides of the opening and firmly pinch closed, as before.

16.

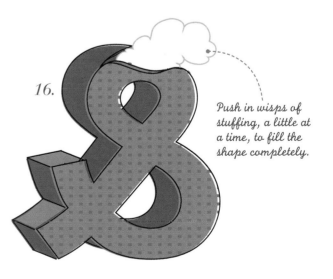

Push in wisps of stuffing, a little at a time, to fill the shape completely.

{Language} Pot Holders

Y ou can't have too many pot holders, and these usefully spell out the warning 'Hot' in French and German as well as English. They're easy to make – the letters are simply machine-stitched outlines filled in with coloured zigzag stitching. The sturdy black denim is repeat-washable, and these will keep looking fresh however tough their kitchen duty.

PERSONALIZING YOUR PROJECT

- Once you've mastered the art of creating a letter outline on the sewing machine and then filling it in with zigzagging stiches, it can be a good way of reproducing some of the more complex/tricky fonts on any textile, from denim to poplin.

ABOUT THE FONT

Seebad

Created by the Swiss designer Silvan Kaeser, and launched commercially in 2003, Seebad was allegedly inspired by some signage seen along the shore of Lake Geneva.

Check out Seebad's unique 'g' to see just how original it is.

FOR THREE POT HOLDERS YOU WILL NEED

Templates on page 123

Thin card to print on (or a laminating machine and glued laminating pouches)

76 x 51 cm (30 x 20 in.) black denim

Three 25.5-cm (10-in.) squares firm iron-on interfacing

Three 25.5-cm (10-in.) squares heat-resistant wadding

Six 100-m (100-yd) reels sewing thread, two in bright pink, two in fluorescent yellow, and two in orange

Black sewing thread

152 cm (60 in.) bias tape, 2.5 cm (1 in.) wide each in bright pink, bright yellow, and bright orange

Craft knife

Sharp scissors

Cutting mat

White gel craft pen

Metal ruler

Compasses

Dressmaker's pins

Making the pot holders

1 Cut a square measuring 23 x 23 cm (9 x 9 in.) from a sheet of paper. Fold it diagonally in both directions and crease sharply, then unfold, so that there is a fold line leading to each corner.

2 Use the ruler to set the compasses to 4 cm (1½ in.) and place the point about 5.4 cm (2⅛ in.) up and away from a corner and draw a rounded corner. Repeat on two of the other corners and cut around the lines, so that the paper square has three rounded and one squared corner.

3 Copy or scan the templates on page 123, enlarging them to scale, print them and cut them out. Either copy them on to thin card to use as templates or put your paper through a laminating machine in light glued pouches.

4 Use the craft knife and metal ruler on a cutting mat to cut out the words to form a stencil. Where the letters have centres, leave small tabs of card to hold them in place.

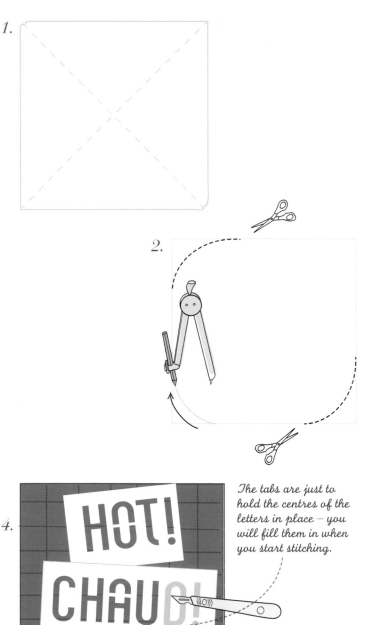

1.

2.

4.

The tabs are just to hold the centres of the letters in place – you will fill them in when you start stitching.

5 Cut six 25.5-cm (10-in.) squares from the black denim. Use a hot iron to press a square of interfacing on to the backs of three of them.

6 Use the gel pen to draw around the paper pattern on one of the pieces of interfaced denim, then position the first word stencil within the outline as shown and draw in the outlines of the letters. Repeat with the second and third word stencils.

7 Thread the sewing machine with the bright yellow thread and stitch carefully around the outlines of the letters of 'CHAUD!', including the exclamation mark. When you've completed the outlines once, sew around them a second time; you may find it easier to turn the machine by hand to keep the stitching exactly on the lines as you go around the curves.

8 Switch the machine's setting to zigzag and practise on a scrap of denim to find the width of stitch you will need to fill in your letters with two or three rows of zigzag stitch. The words 'CHAUD!' and 'HEIß!' can be filled with two rows; 'HOT!' is larger, so will need three rows to fill. Carefully stitch within the letters for 'CHAUD!' until they are completely filled in. To fill in the dot at the base of the exclamation mark, you'll find it easier to combine zigzag with running stitch. Repeat the same process for the other two holders, using a different colour of thread for each.

6.

7.

Stitch the letter outlines very slowly to keep them lean and precise.

8.

9.

9 Cut around the pattern outline for all three pieces of embroidered denim. Cut out the three remaining pieces for the backs of the pot holders, too, remembering to reverse the pattern.

10 Draw around the pattern three times on the squares of heat-resistant wadding and cut them out.

11 Place a plain denim back right side down on your work surface, with a piece of wadding and the 'Chaud!' front right side up on top, aligning the edges, and pin all three layers together.

11.

12 Thread the machine with pink thread and, using a large running stitch, sew around the pot holder, stitching through all three layers 6 mm (¼ in.) in from the edge. Remove the pins.

13 Open out one side of the pink bias binding and, starting at the non-rounded corner, pin it around the edge of the pot holder, flush with the edge. Place the pins at 90 degrees to the edge – this means that you can stitch straight over them. Leave the excess binding on at the end; this will form the hanging loop.

13.

Take in the extra fullness on the corners as you pin the tape on.

14 Turn the pot holder over, fold the loose edge of the bias binding over to the back and pin in place.

15 Place the pot holder front facing upwards in the machine, and stitch around the edge of the bias binding, going through all three layers. When you get to the top left-hand corner, continue to stitch the excess length of binding in half.

16 Use the excess binding to make a 5-cm (2-in.) loop, and tuck the raw end over at the back of the pot holder, on top of the bias strip. Stitch backwards and forwards on the machine to secure along the previous line of stitching on the binding. Finish off the thread.

17 Repeat steps 11–16 to complete the other two pot holders. Use contrasting colours for letters and tape for each, following the photograph.

14.

15.

Stitch to the loose end of the folded binding beyond the corner.

16.

This mobile phone case uses Rosewood, an elaborate font which works best in limited quantities. A single initial – and particularly one that lights up in its translucent window when the phone rings – is a perfect application for it. Choose brightly contrasting shades for the letter and the case for the best effect.

PERSONALIZING YOUR PROJECT

- Dramatic fonts like Rosewood offer you the potential for two-colour letters.
- While we have printed the font on to paper, it can also work well as a crisp appliqué, either in felt or a lighter, but still non-fray, fabric.

ABOUT THE FONT

Although it was only released by Adobe in 1994, Rosewood, designed by Carol Twombly, Carl Crossgrove and Kim Buker Chansler, was inspired by Clarendon Ornamented, a complex display font widely used in the 1880s.

There's plenty of impact in the heavy and elaborate outline of even a single character of Rosewood.

Rosewood is what's technically known as a chromatic, or multicoloured, font.

Making the mobile phone case

1 Use the cloth tape measure to measure around your mobile phone both width- and lengthways. Take the measurements precisely, without any slack in the tape measure.

2 Halve the width measurement and add 12 mm (½ in.) in total for the seam allowances. Using the metal ruler and the craft knife, cut a strip this width from the craft foam, then trim it to the length measurement.

3 Size your initial letter so that it is 4 cm (1½ in.) narrower than the width of your foam strip. Print it in colour on your tracing paper (if you don't have a colour printer, a print shop can do this for you). Cut it out, leaving 6 mm (¼ in.) all around the letter. Cut a second piece of tracing paper the same size.

4 Align the plain piece of tracing paper behind the lettered piece, place them in the top of the laminator pouch, then laminate them in the machine.

5 Cut the letter out, leaving 2 mm (¹⁄₁₆ in.) all around the edge of the paper.

2.

If you've not worked with craft foam or laminated paper before, it's worth spending a bit of time practising cutting and sewing with them before you start on the project itself.

3.

4.

The laminator will coat your letter in plastic to make it sturdy.

6 Using the letter as a template, cut a window in the centre of an A4 sheet of paper. The window needs to be very slightly smaller than the tracing paper, so that it overlaps the edges of the letter piece a little.

7 Draw a line lightly in pencil across the width of your foam piece halfway down the long sides. Draw a second line across the width of your foam halfway between the top edge and the first line. Draw a third line from the centre of the top edge down to the centre of the first line.

8 Fold the paper window pattern in half both lengthways and widthways. Lay it over the foam, with the lengthways and widthways folds aligning with the second and third pencil lines on the foam respectively.

9 Mark the corners of the window on the foam with pencil, join the lines with a ruler and use a ruler and a craft knife to cut the window out of the foam.

10 Position your letter behind the window and stick it in place right on the edge of the window with masking tape, leaving about a 4 mm (⅛ in.) gap all around uncovered, where the window overlaps the foam (this is where the letter will be stitched to the foam), and then adding more tape to the centre of the letter.

6.

Try the letter behind the window to make sure there's a slight overlap.

7.

10.

11 Thread the sewing machine with matching thread. With the front of the letter facing upwards in the machine, slowly stitch around the edge of the window, stitching 2 mm (1/16 in.) from the edge.

12 Peel the masking tape off the back of the window. Pull the threads through to the wrong side of the foam and tie them off, then use a needle to stitch the ends into the machine stitches to secure.

13 Cut the length of cotton tape in half. Use pins to hold one half taut on a piece of corrugated cardboard or a craft workboard and stick a length of double-sided tape along it.

14 Peel off the backing paper from the double-sided tape, then unpin the cotton tape and stick it along the top edge of the foam strip, leaving a short length overhanging at the right-hand edge.

12.

Practise stitching on a scrap of foam before sewing around the frame – turn the wheel manually and set the machine to a long stitch.

13.

14.

15 Turn the foam strip over so that the wrong side is facing upward, fold the short overhanging length over the edge, and secure it down, then align and secure the long remaining piece of tape along the back top edge. Trim the end of the tape at the edge of the foam.

16 Repeat steps 14 and 15 to bind the lower end of the foam strip with the second length of cotton tape in the same way.

17 With the foam strip right side up in the sewing machine and using a long stitch and sewing slowly, as before, sew around the taped ends of the foam. When you've finished, knot the threads and sew the ends into the edge of the tape by hand.

18 Fold the foam strip in half to make the case. Pin the cotton tapes at the top together. Carefully machine stitch down the sides, 2 mm (1/16 in.) in from the edges, reverse stitching at the start and finish of each seam to secure. Knot the threads, stitch them to the inside of the case by hand and cut the ends off.

17.

Turn the ends of the tape in and stitch them down completely.

18.

Even – or perhaps particularly – in the age of the smartphone, there's something special about a photograph album created to mark a memorable trip. This example was made in the colours of the Italian flag to commemorate a visit to Naples, but you can customize your version in whatever way is appropriate to your holiday.

PERSONALIZING YOUR PROJECT

- Anna is used here as a stencil, but would also lend itself particularly well to letters made from binding or tape, with its angled crossbars and sharp, folded corners.

ABOUT THE FONT

ANNA

Named for the daughter of its designer, Daniel Pelavin, Anna was first used on his wedding invitation. Designed in 1991, this uppercase-only font has a rather 1920s appeal – it would seem quite at home on an Art Deco cinema canopy.

Much of the character of Anna comes from its low and sharp-edged crossbars.

YOU WILL NEED

Small photograph album; ours measured around
15 x 20 cm (6 x 8 in.)

Laminating machine and laminating pouches

Sheet of brown paper

White cotton fabric; for our album we required
76 x 12.5 cm (30 x 5 in.)

Two 31-cm (12-in.) squares of
corrugated cardboard

Sheets of white paper

Red fabric paint

Polyurethane washing-up sponge

Fusible bonding web; for our album we required
76 x 12.5 cm (30 x 5 in.)

Firm iron-on interfacing; for our album we
required 76 x 20 cm (30 x 8 in.)

Thin green cotton fabric; for our album we
required 76 x 20 cm (30 x 8 in.)

Green sewing thread

Craft knife

Cloth tape measure

Metal ruler

Dressmaker's pins

Making the album cover

1 Assemble the word and date you want on your album and print them out to scale. The country or city name is about 4.5 cm (1¾ in.) high, and the date is about 3 cm (1⅛ in.). Laminate the name and date using the laminating machine and a glued pouch.

2 Using the craft knife and a metal ruler, cut out the letters and numbers. Cut out the holes in any characters or numbers such as '0', 'A' or 'P', but keep them to one side; you can pin them in position on the stencil later.

3 Use the tape measure to measure the height and the thickness at the top and bottom of the photo album. Add 3 mm (⅛ in.) to this overall measurement.

4 To make the pattern for the album cover, cut a long strip of brown paper to the height worked out in step 3. Wrap it around the album to calculate the length: it should wrap right around the outside of the album and extend inside the front and back covers to just over half the album's width. Cut the brown paper strip to the right length.

2.

If you can choose a relatively short word, your album cover will have more impact.

3.

4.

5 Unfold the cover pattern. Cut the strip of white cotton into two lengths a little longer than required – one for the name and one for the date. The name strip should extend from at least the full width of the back flap to just beyond the right-hand edge of the front cover; the date strip should extend from at least two-thirds of the way across the front cover to the full width of the front flap.

6 Place the two squares of corrugated cardboard, one on top of the other, on your work surface and place some sheets of plain paper on top of them. Lay the right-hand end of the strip of white cotton for the word (in this case, 'Napoli') on top of this, then use pins to fix the word stencil on to it, pinning through to the card. Pin down any cut-out centres of letters, too, using two pins each to prevent them rotating.

7 Cut a small piece of foam from the washing-up sponge, a little wider than the lines of the stencil. Pour a very small quantity of the fabric paint on to a scrap of laminated paper and dab the sponge around in it until it is evenly covered. Dab it on a spare corner of paper to get rid of any excess, then gently dab it on to the stencil, building up the paint until the colour is solid. Repeat with the date stencil on the second strip of cotton, positioning the date near the left-hand end of the strip of cotton.

8 Fix the fabric paint with a hot iron, following the manufacturer's instructions.

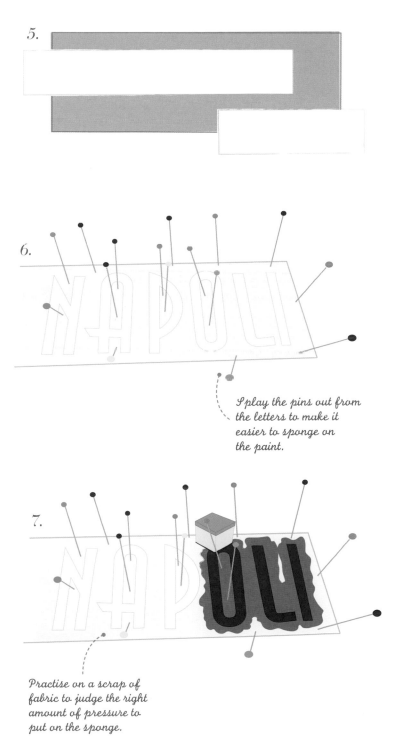

5.

6.

Splay the pins out from the letters to make it easier to sponge on the paint.

7.

Practise on a scrap of fabric to judge the right amount of pressure to put on the sponge.

9 Following the manufacturer's instructions, apply fusible bonding web to the back of the cotton strips.

10 Using a craft knife and a metal ruler, trim the edges of fabric strips so that they are parallel and evenly spaced around the lettering and the date. Cut a straight edge at the end of the word ('Napoli') and at the beginning of the date.

11 Press the iron-on interfacing on to the piece of coloured cotton fabric. Lay the paper pattern on the wrong side of the fabric and draw around it, adding a 12-mm (½-in.) seam allowance on the two long sides. Cut out the fabric.

12 Fold the fabric around the album, making sure that the short sides are parallel with the edges and that the flaps are the same size. Place the lettered strips in position, aligning them with the album edges and making sure they're parallel with one another, too. When you are happy with their positions, mark their corners with a pencil.

13 Take the fabric off the album, peel off the backing paper from the fusible bonding web, position the strips on the fabric and press in place.

9.

Make sure the edges of the strips are exactly parallel with the edges of the characters.

10.

12.

14 Fold the short ends of the fabric over by 12 mm (½ in.) and press flat. Thread the sewing machine with green thread and stitch the raw edges down.

15 Wrap the fabric round the album again, making sure that the flaps are the same size. On the outside of the cover, mark the points where the flaps end.

16 Take the fabric off. With right sides together, fold the flaps back to the marked points on the outside of the cover and pin in place. Machine stitch along the top and bottom edges of the flaps, 12 mm (½ in.) from the raw edges, reverse stitching at the start and finish to secure. Snip off the corners, close to the seam.

17 Turn the cover right side out, pushing out the corners with scissor points or the tip of a pencil. Press flat, then turn under the 12-mm (½-in.) seam allowances along the top and bottom edges and press them flat.

18 Right side up, topstitch a line along the top and bottom edges of the album cover, 1–2 mm (¹⁄₁₆ in.) from the edge, reverse stitching at the start and finish.

19 Put the cover on the album. Any puckers or wrinkles can be gently pressed out by using a warm iron through a clean tea towel.

14.

16.

Trimming the corners will ensure sharp corners when the cover is turned the right way out.

18.

The zippy, upbeat look of this font is reminiscent of signwriting and is perfectly suited to the kitchen – if you argue with your co-chef, at least you can make sure that your apron agrees with you! The letters are quite elaborate but you'll find the stencil relatively easy to cut, especially if you use a laminating machine to make it. If you live in a household with a lot of keen cooks, you could make a matching set of aprons with different-coloured stripes and an appropriate phrase for each one. Before you start, test the paints on the fabrics you intend to use to check that the paint doesn't bleed.

PERSONALIZING YOUR PROJECT

- With script fonts like this, plan out your word or phrase and experiment with different sizes to get the best balance for your project.
- Candy Script has a variety of different forms for each character in the alphabet, allowing you to create a range of looks with the same font.

ABOUT THE FONT

Created in 2007 by the Argentinian type designer Alejandro Paul, Candy Script was invented to celebrate the hand-painted signage seen all over South America.

Check the variety of letterforms available if you want to create your own message – you'll often find two or three variants.

YOU WILL NEED

Template on page 124
Plain calico apron
Two 25-ml pots bright red fabric paint
25-ml pot navy-blue fabric paint
Laminating machine and laminating pouch
Few sheets of plain paper
Two 31-cm (12-in.) squares of corrugated card
Polyurethane washing-up sponge
28-cm (11-in.) square of mid-weight white cotton fabric (for the lettered patch)
28-cm (11-in.) square of fusible bonding web
White sewing thread
Craft knife
Sharp scissors
Cutting mat
Red pencil
2.5-cm (1-in.) paintbrush
1-m (1-yd) metal ruler
Dressmaker's pins

Making the apron

1 Press your apron flat and lay it on a flat surface. Use the ruler to find the centre point of the bib and draw a vertical centre line all the way down the apron with red pencil.

2 Mark two more lines 2.5 cm (1 in.) either side of the centre line – these outer two lines mark the width of the central red stripe (5 cm/2 in.). Continue to work outwards from the centre line, marking red stripes that are 5 cm (2 in.) wide 2.5 cm and (1 in.) apart.

3 Shake the red fabric paint thoroughly before you open the pot. Lay the apron on a flat surface protected with several layers of newspaper and paint the red stripes following the pencil lines. Don't be too careful with the edges; the end effect is supposed to look hand-painted.

4 Fix the paint with a hot iron, following the manufacturer's instructions.

5 Copy or scan the template on page 124, enlarging it to scale, and print it out. Laminate the print-out in the laminator. Use a craft knife on a cutting mat to cut the letters out to create a stencil. Cut out the centres of both 'Es', but retain the pieces so that they can be pinned in place when you're using the stencil.

2.

3.

Work quite quickly so that the fabric paint doesn't dry before you finish and leave you with a patchy effect.

5.

6 Lay out the two squares of corrugated card, one on top of the other, then lay a couple of layers of plain paper on top, and finally the mid-weight cotton fabric square.

7 Pin the stencil on to the cotton, pushing the pins through the cotton and paper and into the cardboard to hold them in place. Place the pins as shown, pointing outwards from the holes in the stencil (this will make it easier to sponge the paint in place). Pin the centres of the 'Es' in place with two upright pins so that the centres won't rotate.

8 Cut a piece of foam from the washing-up sponge, just a tiny bit wider than the lines of the letters.

9 Shake the navy-blue fabric paint thoroughly, then open the pot and pour a little on to a scrap of the laminated paper. Dab the sponge around in it until it is evenly covered, then dab it up and down on a paint-free piece of paper to remove any excess. Dab the sponge gently through the stencil, building up the colour until the letter areas are solidly coloured.

7.

Check that the pins' positioning allows you to reach all parts of the stencil before you start to paint.

8.

Try to cut the sponge block in quite an even shape — you'll find it easier to use.

9.

10 Leave the paint to dry before removing the stencil from the fabric, then fix the fabric paint with a hot iron, following the manufacturer's instructions.

11 Print out a second copy of the template and cut around the speech bubble. Press the square of fusible bonding web on to the back of the lettered patch. Place the template on top of the lettered patch and draw around the speech bubble using a pencil, then cut it out.

12 Make sure the apron is laying flat. Peel the paper backing off the bonding web and position the speech bubble on the front of the apron, then lay a tea towel over it and iron the patch on, following the manufacturer's instructions.

13 For a neat finish, thread the sewing machine with white thread and sew around the edge of the patch with a zigzag stitch.

Stitching the edge in a zigzag will make the patch sturdier as well as looking neat.

{Picnic} Blanket

P VC sheeting is available in plenty of summery, upbeat patterns that combine well with a bold, simple bit of font application to make your personal take on a waterproof picnic blanket. Keep it in the car boot so that you can indulge al fresco when the sun's shining but the grass is still damp.

PERSONALIZING YOUR PROJECT

- The broad shapes of Stone Sans make it ideal if you're not confident about cutting narrow links on letters. It works well at most scales, and makes for simply stencil cutting.

ABOUT THE FONT

Stone Sans

Named for its designer, Sumner Stone, Stone Sans is part of a font family he created in 1987, when he was Director of Typography for Adobe. Solid but stylish, it cooperates well with other fonts, but this project showcases it working solo.

YOU WILL NEED

1.5 m (60 in.) patterned PVC table-covering fabric, 140 cm (55 in.) wide

1 m (39 in.) spunbound nonwoven polypropylene fabric, 150 cm (59 in.) wide; if you can't find this, use a plain-coloured PVC table-covering fabric

1.5 m (60 in.) ripstop fabric, rubber-backed if possible, 150 cm (59 in.) wide

6 m (6½ yds) cotton bias tape, 2.5 cm (1 in.) wide

Sewing thread to match the PVC, ripstop and bias tape

Scissors

Fine marker or ballpoint pen

Pencil

Tape measure

Masking tape

Dressmaker's pins

The forms of Stone Sans are often quirkier than they first appear — here, look at the joins on the 'K' or the curl of the 'P'.

Making the blanket

1 Measure the width of the patterned PVC and cut the length to match, so that you have a square piece (PVC is usually available in 140-cm/55-in. widths). If it is creased from storage, you can relax the folds and flatten it with a hairdryer set to warm.

2 Print out your letters, with the tallest (in our case, the 'p') enlarged so that it is 48 cm (19 in.) high. For some letters you may need to use multiple sheets of paper that you combine after printing. Cut the letters out; in our case we needed to record the distance between the stem of the 'i' and its dot so that we could position them correctly later.

3 Draw around the paper patterns on the polypropylene and cut them out.

4 Find the centre point of your PVC, then work out the positioning for your letters, so that they appear in two even lines in the middle of the sheet. For each line, lay a tape measure along where the base of the letters (without the 'tails') should sit, then stick short pieces of masking tape on the PVC, using the tape measure as a guide, to mark the position for each letter.

Move the hairdryer quickly around the creased areas until the PVC relaxes.

1.

2.

Align the sections of letter before taping sheets of paper together, and place the tape where it won't be cut off.

4.

Using short pieces of tape prevents the 'tails' getting in the way when removing the tape later on.

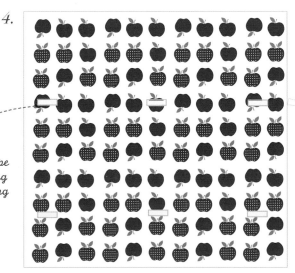

5 Starting with the central polypropylene letter on the top row (in our case, 'i'), tape it in place on the PVC using little tabs of masking tape.

6 Thread your sewing machine with thread to match the polypropylene and, using a large zigzag stitch, sew around the letter. You'll find it easiest to do each character in two halves (so you're not trying to push the whole bulk of the PVC through the machine at any point) and to roll it up either side of each letter as you stitch, so you don't have to work with the whole size of the sheet. When you turn corners in the letters, leave the needle down in the polypropylene fabric as you turn. Knot the threads at the back of the PVC. Repeat steps 5 and 6 for the remaining letters.

7 Lay the ripstop fabric on the floor, wrong side up, and lay the PVC fabric on top of it, right side up. Use tabs of masking tape to stick the PVC down on to the ripstop.

8 Thread the sewing machine with thread to match the ripstop and stitch around the two layers, 6 mm (¼ in.) in from the edge of the PVC. Trim the ripstop to the edge of the PVC.

9 Thread the sewing machine with thread to match the cotton bias tape. Begin attaching the tape, halfway along one side of the blanket, by first turning the end of the tape down at a 45-degree angle, as shown, before stitching.

5.

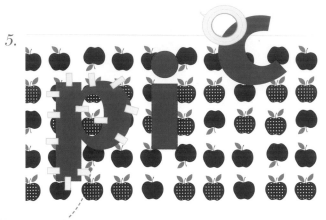

You can peel the tape pieces off the letters as you machine them.

7.

9.

10 Stop the machine 4 cm (1½ in.) from the corner of the blanket. Fold the tape at a right angle, moving the tape away from the blanket and aligned to the bottom of the PVC, then fold it back on itself to run along the adjoining edge of the blanket. Now fold the 'triangle flap' at the corner down and continue stitching to the crease in the fold, then finish the stitches by making a few stitches backwards and forwards.

11 Take the blanket out of the machine and start stitching again on the other side of the fold 1 cm (½ in.) from the edge of the tape folded underneath. Continue in this way until you return to the starting point. Snip off any excess tape just beyond where you stop stitching. Go backwards and forwards for a few stitches to secure the end.

12 Fold the bias tape over to the back of the blanket, enclosing the edges of the blanket. Begin pinning down the bias tape along one edge, covering the stitches.

13 At the corner, after pinning the bias in place along one edge, fold over the adjoining edge, which should form a neat mitred corner. Pin in place, then continue until the bias is pinned down all around. Stitch it down neatly, sewing just inside the inner edge of the tape.

After one edge is pinned down, turn the tape at the corner over to make a mitred fold with straight edges.

10.

12.

13.

{Leather & Canvas} Shopper

This shopper is solidly made from a mix of thin leather and heavyweight drill, with durable rope handles. Franklin Gothic has supplied the necessary bold letter for the appliqué, to make the best use of the red/green colour contrast, and sans serif suits the clean shape well, but the simplicity of the design means that you could adapt pretty much any font or letter according to taste. If you're not used to topstitching on your machine, experiment on scraps of drill and leather before you put the bag together.

PERSONALIZING YOUR PROJECT

• Even, solid and straightforward to cut out, this font is a good pick for projects using letters that need to be readable at a distance.

ABOUT THE FONT

FRANKLIN GOTHIC

Issued by American Type Founders in 1902, and designed by one of the early twentieth century's star typographers, Morris Fuller Benton, Franklin Gothic was an immediate hit and has been one of the most widely used sans serif fonts ever since.

YOU WILL NEED

40 cm (15½ in.) heavy cotton drill in a natural colour, 147 cm (58 in.) wide

51-cm (20-in.) square green leather

Piece of thin red leather or leatherette (check your letter template for size before buying)

Sewing thread in red

Top stitch thread in green and cream

Four silver eyelets with washers, 11 mm (⁷⁄₁₆ in.) in diameter

2 m (2 yds) twisted rope cord, 8 mm (⁵⁄₁₆ in.) in diameter

Leather sewing machine needle

Denim sewing machine needle

Eyelet maker

Sharp scissors

Non-permanent fabric marker pen

Pencil

Hi-tack craft glue

Tape measure

Masking tape

Dressmaker's pins

Undramatic but distinctive, the Franklin Gothic family offers a whole range of compressed and condensed weights – so it's also a good choice if you want to fit a word into a tight space in a project.

Making the shopper

1 Cut out two rectangles from the cotton drill, each measuring 49 x 27 cm (19 x 10½ in.). Cut out one rectangle from the green leather, measuring 49 x 43 cm (19 x 17 in.).

2 Machine stitch around the edges of the drill rectangles, using zigzag stitch to stop them from fraying.

3 Place a cotton drill rectangle on each 49-cm (19-in.) side of the leather. Run a fine line of hi-tack craft glue along the sides of the two cotton drill rectangles abutting the leather and stick the leather down on to the cotton drill, overlapping it by about 12 mm (½ in.). Leave to dry.

4 Thread the sewing machine with green top stitch thread and, using a leather needle, run a large zigzag stitch along each glued seam of the leather.

1.

Test your scissors for sharpness before you cut the leather – you need some that are relatively heavy and very sharp.

3.

4.

5 Print out your letter, enlarged to 25.5 cm (10 in.) tall, and cut it out.

6 Fold the drill/leather rectangle in half lengthways, wrong sides together, and use a tape measure and a non-permanent fabric marker pen to find and mark the centre point of the rectangle's width. Unfold the rectangle.

7 Place your paper letter template at the centre point and position it so that the base of the template falls about 10 cm (4 in.) below the edge of the leather. When you've got your template straight, mark the corners of the template on to the drill and leather using a non-permanent fabric marker pen.

8 Use the paper pattern to draw around and cut out your letter from the thin red leather. Stick it in place on the side of the bag using hi-tack craft glue, using the guide points you drew in the previous step. Leave to dry.

7.

The marks will ensure that you place the 'N' correctly.

8.

9 Using the leather needle on the sewing machine and red thread, zigzag stitch around the letter.

10 Fold the rectangle in half again, this time right sides together, and machine stitch the side seams, using a running stitch and stitching 12 mm (½ in.) in from the edges. Reverse stitch for about 2.5 cm (1 in.) at the beginning and end of each seam to strengthen it.

11 To make the corners and give the bag a flat base, fold the bag as shown in the diagram so that the side seams are aligned in the centre and the corners of the leather stick out in a triangle at the bottom.

12 Open out the leather seam of one of the corners and tape it down, open, with two strips of masking tape. Using a ruler and a non-permanent fabric marker pen, mark a line at 90 degrees to the seam and 12.5 cm (5 in.) long from edge to edge.

9.

Align the zigzag stitches exactly along the edge of the leather letter for the neatest finish.

11.

12.

Press the corner of the bag down firmly before marking the cross line.

13 Thread your machine with green thread and, using a leather needle, stitch along the drawn line, reverse stitching for about 2.5 cm (1 in.) at the beginning and end of the seam to strengthen it. Cut off the corner 1 cm (⅜ in.) below the stitching. Repeat on the other corner of the bag.

14 Mark a pencil line 5 cm (2 in.) down from the raw edge of the drill on the wrong side, then fold the raw edge down to meet the line and press the crease with a hot iron. Turn the edge down again, so that you have a double fold, and press again.

15 Thread your machine with cream thread and, using a denim needle, stitch along the turned-under edge 6 mm (¼ in.) in from the fold.

16 Turn the bag right side out and mark the centre top of each side with a pin. Using a non-permanent marker pen, make a mark 10 cm (4 in.) either side of the centre mark on each side. Use the eyelet maker to set the eyelets in place at each marked point, 1 cm (⅜ in.) down from the top edge of the bag.

17 Cut the rope cord in half and make the handles, tying tight knots on the inside of the bag to hold them secure.

13.

14.

16.

Make sure the eyelets are in line with one another as well as with the edge of the bag.

{Calligraphic} Table Runner

The vivid yellow of the linen in this project sets off the grey herringbone of the scripted message beautifully. The script is made from bias tape, appliquéd on to the linen; cutting the tape on the bias makes it stretchy, which makes it easier to pull the pieces into shape to match the flowing curves of the type. This project is probably a little more challenging than some others in the book, so do set aside a few evenings to make it. After making your own bias tape in two different widths, you need to follow the diagram to apply short pieces in a certain order – but it's satisfying to see the curves begin to echo the font very exactly.

PERSONALIZING YOUR PROJECT

- If you choose your own phrase, you will find that the letters are thicker than your bias tape, so just use the tape around the outside edge of each letter.

ABOUT THE FONT

Santa Fe

Designed in the 1980s by the British designer David Quay, Santa Fe's curling shapes, elaborately rounded characters and forward slant all give it an appealing go-faster feel.

The rather fluid character forms of Santa Fe are more legible in script than as individual letters.

YOU WILL NEED

Template on pages 124–5

2.5-cm (1-in.) and 12-mm (½-in.) bias tape makers

2 m (2 yd) bright yellow linen, 147 cm (58 in.) wide

1 m (1 yd) thin, tight-woven herringbone fabric, 147 cm (58 in.) wide, in shades of brown, for the lettering; if you use another fabric, pick a thin but tight weave, such as a lightweight suiting material

Brown sewing thread to match font fabric

Embroidery needle

Embroidery hoop, 25.5 cm (10 in.) in diameter

1-m (1-yd) metal ruler

Craft knife

Sharp scissors

Cutting mat

Non-permanent fabric marker pen

Tape measure

Masking tape

Dressmaker's pins

Making the table runner

1 Copy or scan the template on pages 124–5, enlarging it to scale. You will need to print it out on to several sheets of paper, so tape them together to make a single pattern.

2 Cut out the type neatly with a craft knife to make a stencil.

3 Follow the manufacturer's instructions on the bias tape maker to make two lengths of bias tape from the brown herringbone fabric cut on the bias – 4.5 m (5 yd) of 2.5-cm (1-in.) wide tape and 5.5 m (6 yd) of 12-mm (½-in.) wide tape. You will be using it in short pieces, so there is no need to join the strips together when you have cut them. The 12-mm (½-in.) tape will be used for the lettering and the 2.5-cm (1-in.) tape will be used for the binding around the edge of the runner.

4 Cut a 50-cm (19½-in.) strip from the linen. Press the remaining linen so that it is crease free and stick it to your work surface with masking tape. Find and mark the mid-point of the fabric's length. Lay the paper stencil over the fabric, matching the mid-points (the mid-point of the stencil should be the top of the vertical of the first 'p' in 'appétit').

1.

Tape the paper front and back to strengthen the joins.

3.

Simply pull the fabric strips through the tape maker – it does the work for you.

You will need to add strip 3 before you lay out the curved section of strip 1.

4.

5 Pin the stencil to the linen and draw around it using the non-permanent fabric marker pen. Use a ruler to extend the lines that run from the base of the initial 'B' and the exclamation mark. Remove the tape from the linen so that you can start to stitch the lettering.

5.

6 The letters are pieced together from the short lengths of bias tape cut in step 3. The order in which the tape is applied is shown in the diagram on the previous page: look carefully at the diagram as you go, as it makes the order of stitching clear by showing which pieces of tape overlay others. Start with the 'B', taking one of the longer pieces of the 12-mm (½-in.) tape (it needs to be long enough to complete the letter). Pin the tape in from the left-hand side of the linen to just before the vertical of the 'B'.

6.

7 Using ladder stitch, sew the bottom edge of the tape down to the point at which the vertical of the 'B' starts, then cut a piece of tape to make the vertical, leaving enough spare tape at the end to fold it down. Pin the vertical in position and place the linen in an embroidery hoop, pulling tight, to stitch it.

8 Stitch the vertical, using ladder stitch, then continue with a short length to join the 'B' and the 'o'; this needs to be sewn before you complete the 'B', as shown on the diagram. Stitch the outside edges before the inside edges.

8.

The embroidery hoop will hold the area you're working on taut as you fold the tape around the curves.

9 When you have sewn the linking piece (marked 3 on the diagram), complete the curves of the 'B'. You will need to make a fold in the tape between the two curves.

10 Remove the linen from the embroidery hoop and press it, then put the hoop back, moving it to the right on the linen so that you can complete working on the 'o'.

11 Take a length of tape long enough for the whole of the 'o', the link between the 'o' and the 'n', and the upright stroke of the 'n'. Pin the tape in place over the word outline and stitch around the outer edge of the 'o', making a tuck where shown on the stitching diagram.

12 Sew the inside edge of the 'o' and stitch down the tuck. Stitch up the left side of the tape that makes the upright of the 'n'. Tuck in the end of the upright and stitch down.

13 Move the embroidery hoop so that it contains the whole of the letter 'n'. Cut a piece of tape to make the rest of the 'n', cut the end at an angle, and tuck it into the open right-hand side of the upright. Stitch down the right-hand side of the upright.

9.

11.

Pin every character completely, taking in the extra fabric on the curves, before you start to stitch.

13.

14 Pin and stitch the remainder of the 'n' along the outside edge, making a tuck at the base of the curve, as shown on the stitching diagram. Turn in the raw end and stitch, then sew the inside edge of the 'n'.

15 Continue following the stitching diagram in the same way to complete 'appétit!', moving the embroidery hoop to the right as necessary and pressing the linen between characters. Stitch the tape to run off the linen from the full point of the exclamation mark, stitching the end down at the edge of the linen.

16 Tape the linen back to your work surface. The runner will measure 178 by 32 cm (70 by 12½ in.) long. Measuring from the centre mark, trim the four sides ready to bind around the edges.

17 Take one end of the 2.5-cm (1-in.) tape and open it out, laying it face down on the right side of the runner starting halfway up one of the short edges. Turn the end of the tape over at a 45-degree angle (see step 9, page 84), before stitching. Tack the binding in place up to the corner of the runner.

18 Mitre the corners of the runner as you tack, folding the bias tape away from the fabric at right angles to make an L-shape when you reach a corner, and then folding it back down on itself along the adjoining edge and pinning it in place.

14.

16.

Press the runner lightly before trimming the edges to straight lines at each end.

18.

19 When you have tacked the tape all around the runner, thread the sewing machine with matching thread and stitch the tape in place, sewing along the first fold line of the tape. See steps 10 and 11 on page 85 for instructions on stitching at the corner.

20 Press the tape from the front of the runner, using a steam iron. At the corners, press 45-degree folds with the tape from the long sides of the runner on top of the fold.

21 Turn the runner over and fold the tape over to the back of the runner, pressing the short ends so that the edge of the tape aligns with the line of stitching.

22 Press the tape on the long sides of the runner on the back, making folds in the corners. Stitch the corners down by hand, then sew along the length of the tape using a small ladder stitch.

20.

21.

When pressed, the tape will turn neatly over the edge of the runner, ready to be stitched down on the back.

22.

The best-ever handmade way to mark a big occasion or send a special message, you only need to master a basic pennant structure to customize these bunting garlands. Our 'Happy New Year' materials allow for twelve letters, but you can size up or down to make any message you want. We've used a clean-cut inline font: the internal line within each letter, along with a contrasting colour of surround, ensures it reads easily at a distance.

PERSONALIZING YOUR PROJECT

- Inline letters look clean and crisp, but for obvious reasons, it's near-impossible to reproduce the whole characters as stencils. For fabric, they work best with appliquéd bias tape.

ABOUT THE FONT

CYCLONE

Designed by Hoefler & Frere-Jones, based in New York, Cyclone is a slightly elongated inline font. There are alternatives for six characters to enable you to change the mood visually.

MnoyX

Try black and white as well as colourful mixes — monochromatic in contrasting materials will look good.

YOU WILL NEED

Templates on page 127

1 m (1 yd) mid-weight fusible bonding web

20-cm (8-in.) square each of bright pink, turquoise and yellow felt

Two 20-cm (8-in.) squares of orange felt

61 cm (24 in.) blue silk, 115 cm (45 in.) wide

61 cm (24 in.) green silk, 115 cm (45 in.) wide

Sewing thread in pink, blue, green, turquoise, yellow and orange

6 m (6½ yds) gimp braid, 6 mm (¼ in.) wide

6 m (6½ yds) bias tape, 2.5 cm (1 in.) wide

Craft knife and cutting mat

Sharp scissors

Hole punch

Non-permanent fabric marker pen

Hi-tack craft glue

Metal ruler

Dressmaker's pins

Making the bunting

1 Make a quick sketch of your words so that you can plan the letter colours. We alternated pink, turquoise, yellow and orange felt, but you could use fewer colours or even stick with just one, if you prefer a simpler effect.

2 Cut out a square of bonding web for each of the felt squares, trimming it to fit the squares exactly, and press with a warm iron to fuse a square bonding web to each of the felt squares.

3 Print out the letters, enlarged to 16 cm (6¼ in.) high, and cut them out neatly to make templates.

4 Reverse your letter templates, lay them on the wrong side of the felt squares and draw around them with a non-permanent fabric marker pen. (Check your plan to make sure that you're cutting each letter from the right colour of felt.)

5 Cut the letters out of the felt. For the neatest finish, cut the straight lines with a metal ruler and a craft knife and the curves with a small, sharp pair of scissors.

1.

4.

Arrange all the letters you need on each piece of felt before drawing around them, to make sure there's enough felt for all the letters.

5.

6 Copy or scan the templates on page 127, enlarging it to scale, print it and cut it out. Cut 12 flag shapes from the blue silk and 10 from the green using the smaller template, adding a 2.5-cm (1-in.) seam allowance around each shape. Cut 2 flag shapes from the green silk using the wider template for the 'W' (it needs more room than the other letters), adding a 2.5-cm (1-in.) seam allowance around each shape.

7 Fold the template along the vertical fold line, place it on the front of a flag shape and use the non-permanent marker pen to mark a vertical line down the flag, then unfold. Now, fold the template down at the horizontal fold line and mark this line on the flag. Mark six of the blue and six of the green flag shapes in this way.

8 Peel the backing paper off the felt letters and centre them on the prepared flag shapes along the vertical line and below the horizontal line, matching the colours to the plan and using the marker lines as placement guides.

9 Press the letters on to the flag pieces with a warm iron, using a clean tea towel between the iron and the fabric.

6.

7.

Lift the iron and replace it on another part of the fabric — don't move it around directly on the fabric.

9.

10 When all the letters are in place, thread the sewing machine with pink thread and stitch around the pink letters with a small zigzag stitch. Rethread the machine with thread in each of the other felt colours in turn and stitch around all the letters.

11 Use the non-permanent marker pen to mark the position for placing the braid inside each felt letter. Use a hole punch – or a pencil will do – to make holes in the letter template along the top and base of each section of the letter and at cross sections, stopping the lines about 12 mm (½ in) short of the ends, depending on the the size of the template.

12 Use a craft knife to cut small slits the width of the braid through both the felt and silk backing at all the pairs of dots on each letter.

13 Now apply the braid to the central line of the letters. Starting with the letter 'H', cut a length of braid 5 cm (2 in.) longer than the central crossline and use the points of scissors to push it through the slits to the back.

14 Insert two pins into the braid where it meets the slits, then pull the braid back up a little, but not out of the slits, and glue the back of the braid between the pins. Pull the ends from the back of the flag so the braid lies flat and leave to dry.

11.

13.

The slits in the felt should be just wide enough to fit the braid flat as you feed it through.

14.

The pins indicate where to apply the glue – remove them once the glue has been applied.

15 To make the sides of the 'H', cut two lengths of braid, each 5 cm (2 in.) longer than the length of the sides. As before, mark the area to be glued with pins, glue the back of each length of braid and stick down. Leave to dry.

16 Push the unglued ends of the braid through to the back of the flag with the points of scissors and glue down all the ends on the back. Repeat steps 13 to 16 for each flag.

17 Place the paper pattern on the back of each lettered flag piece, using the folds to line it up centrally with the letter, then draw around it with the marker.

18 Line up each lettered flag piece with a plain flag the same colour, right sides together. Sew around the side and base edges of the drawn pattern outline, leaving the top open. Trim the seam allowances to 1 cm (½ in.), then turn the flags the right way round and press.

19 Use the ruler and marker pen to draw a line 2.5 cm (1 in.) above the lettering on each of the flags.

20 Cut the bias binding into two equal lengths. Mark the centre point of one piece with a pin, open the tape out and pin the first 'P' of 'HAPPY' in place, along the line drawn on the top edge of the letter. Pin on the rest of the letters, leaving a 2.5-cm (1-in.) gap between each flag.

16.

Use glue very sparingly to stick the braid down.

18.

20.

21 Mark the centre point of the second piece of tape and pin the left-hand corner of the 'Y' of 'YEAR' under it. Add the letters in the same way as before, leaving 2.5-cm (1-in) gaps between them, except between the 'W' and the 'Y', which should have a 7.5-cm (3-in.) gap to mark the space between the words.

22 Machine stitch the tape on to the flags. Trim off the top of each flag just below the edge of the tape.

23 Fold the other side of the tape over the top edge of the flags and press it so that the edge lines up with the existing line of stitching.

24 Stitch along the full length of the tape, taking in the flags as you go (make sure you place the bunting in the machine the right way up). Fold in the raw ends of the tape and stitch closed.

21.

23.

24.

A large-scale monogram transforms an everyday striped duvet cover. This one is confected with a mix of fabric paint and custom-made bias tape and, with its mix of navy and white on a ticking stripe cover, has a neat, nautical effect. It's worth adding to your craft kit by buying a bias tape maker: they're inexpensive and you'll find that homemade bias tape is invaluable in dozens of craft applications. However, if you're time poor or want to keep it simple, you can buy ready-made white bias tape.

PERSONALIZING YOUR PROJECT

• Real grosgrain two-colour ribbon with a single central stripe can be used to re-create inline letters – it's simpler than a combined stencil-and-appliqué approach, although you may not be able to imitate the font precisely.

ABOUT THE FONT

RIBBON

The Philadelphia designer Dan Kneiding created Ribbon for the Lost Type Co-op. The V-cut ends give this uppercase-only font a very distinctive look.

Ribbon is unusual in that the complexity of the different characters varies a lot across the alphabet – see 'A' compared to 'C', for example.

YOU WILL NEED

Sheets of A4 paper to print and copy on; you'll need enough for 3 letters, each 38 cm (15 in.) high

Laminating machine and glued laminating pouch

Cotton or polycotton duvet cover; the blue ticking stripe on the example we used contrasts well with the strong navy monogram, but you could use a plain cover if you prefer and alter the colour of the fabric paint to match or contrast

Sheet of brown paper

A1 sheet of card

Navy fabric paint

76 cm (30 in.) white cotton or polycotton sheeting fabric, 229 cm (7 ft 6 in.) wide, or ready-made white bias tape, 6 mm (¼ in.) wide

6-mm (¼-in.) bias tape maker

White sewing thread

Embroidery needle

Embroidery hoop, 25 cm (10 in.) in diameter

Dark and light chalk pencils plus normal pencil

Wide and narrow paintbrushes

Masking tape

Clear adhesive tape

Metal ruler

Cloth tape measure

Dressmaker's pins

Making the duvet cover

1 Print out your letters, enlarged to 38 cm (15 in.) tall. Place them in the top of the laminator pouch, then laminate them in the machine. Cut out and tape the pieces together.

2 Iron the duvet cover and spread it out on a flat surface.

3 Using the metal ruler and a chalk pencil, draw a line across the duvet 54 cm (21 in.) down from the top edge. Use the tape measure and the ruler to find the centre point of this line and mark it with a chalk pencil.

4 Mark and draw a second line 7.5 cm (3 in.) down from the first, 61 cm (24 in.) from the top edge.

5 Put loops of masking tape on the back of each letter template, so that they can be stuck down on the duvet cover.

6 Position the template for the middle letter of your monogram at the centre point established across the width of the duvet cover, with its top edge aligning with the 54-cm (21-in.) line.

1.

Cut the ribbon points of the stencils very sharply to get the full effect on the finished cover.

4.

Before you start check that you have enough workspace to move around the duvet once it's laid flat.

6.

7 Line up the other letter templates on
either side of the central letter,
aligning the letter tops with the lower
61-cm (24-in.) line on the cover.

8 Draw around the templates with a
sharp normal pencil, then remove
them from the cover.

9 Tape the brown paper over the A1
sheet of card, sticking it down at
the corners.

10 Slip the card inside the duvet
cover, so that it's behind all three
letters of the monogram; this will stop
the fabric paint from bleeding through
to the second layer of the cover. Once it's
in position, don't move it until the letters
are all painted and dry.

11 Use a fine paintbrush and fabric
paint to paint the outlines of the
three letters, then a broader brush to fill
them in. Leave until the paint is completely
dry.

12 Fix the fabric paint with an iron,
following the manufacturer's
instructions. Wash the duvet cover.

8.

11.

Use the fabric paint sparingly; be careful not to overload the brush.

13 Use the tape measure to measure the central, ribbon stripe in each of the monogram's letters. From the white cotton sheeting, cut strips 14 mm (⁹⁄₁₆ in.) wide on the bias and use the tape maker to convert them into bias tape (you can use ready-made tape if you prefer).

14 Cut each of the letter templates into pieces along one side of the stripe/gap in the ribbon font.

15 Iron the washed duvet cover. You will now draw the centre line for each letter using the light chalk pencil by laying pieces of the templates on top of the corresponding painted letter on the duvet. For some letters such as 'S' and 'G', you will just need to use one of the two halves of each template. For more complex letters such as 'W', which divide into more than two pieces, you will need to use some additional pieces.

16 If necessary unpick a small gap in the middle of the top seam of the duvet cover (this is to enable you to get your hand in to stitch on the bias tape).

17 Fix the embroidery hoop around the top of the left-hand letter. Pin the bias tape along the chalked central line on the letter.

13.

15.

Hold the stencil down carefully as you draw the chalk guide lines.

17.

18 Thread an embroidery needle with white thread and ladder stitch the tape down on to the letter, stitching the first side of the tape over the chalk line. Fold under the end of the tape at the top end of the letter and stitch down the other side of the tape.

19 Remove the hoop and repeat step 18 around the lower half of the letter. (For larger characters, such as 'W,' you may need to reposition the hoop several times.)

20 Repeat steps 18 and 19 for the other two letters of the monogram.

21 Lay a clean tea towel over the letters and press them with a warm iron.

22 Slipstitch the gap in the top seam of the duvet cover closed.

18.

A small ladder stitch is best for fixing the tape in place.

20.

22.

{Initialled} Messenger Bag

W hether or not you're a cyclist, the classic messenger bag with its cross-body strap is invaluable for toting all your stuff. This version has everything you'd want: made from thin black leather, with reflective straps and your choice of letter. The initial letter appliqué is both glued and stitched, so will stand up to the toughest treatment.

PERSONALIZING YOUR PROJECT

- We've created a shadow for the letter in this project, but the font looks just as strong without it.
- One of the rare faces with no straight lines, Hobo works well anywhere you want a flowing, organic shape to your type.

ABOUT THE FONT

Hobo

Created in 1910 by the American designer Morris Fuller Benton, Hobo is unusual in that all the characters rest on the same line, with no descenders.

Without descenders, this font is a good pick for any project that calls for characters to share a baseline.

YOU WILL NEED

Templates on pages 126–7
Large sheet of brown paper
Piece of thin black leather, at least 121 x 51 cm (48 x 20 in.)
31-cm (12-in.) square of yellow leatherette
20 x 25.5-cm (8 x 10-in.) piece of white leatherette
13-cm (5-in.) square of black leatherette
13-cm (5-in.) square of grey leatherette
2 m (80 in.) black nylon webbing, 2.5 cm (1 in.) wide
Two black plastic loops to fit webbing
28 cm (11 in.) hook-and-loop tape, 2.5 cm (1 in.) wide
115 cm (45 in.) reflective plastic tape, 2.5 cm (1 in.) wide
Black plastic buckle to fit webbing
Sewing thread in black, white, grey and yellow
Sewing needle
Leather sewing machine needle
Thimble
Sharp scissors
Heavy-duty scissors (to cut leather)
Ballpoint pen
Pencil
Hi-tack craft glue
Latex-based contact adhesive
Small spatula or glue spreader
Masking tape
1-m (1-yd) metal ruler
Straight pins

Making the messenger bag

1 Copy or scan the templates for the pieces of the bag on pages 126–7, enlarging them to scale, then print and cut them out. (You may need several sheets of paper for this; if so, overlap the pieces and tape them together.) Draw around the template pieces on brown paper to make the pattern and cut them out.

2 Copy or scan the templates for the bubbles on page 126, enlarging them to scale, then print and cut them out.

3 Enlarge the letter and full stop you want to use so that they fit easily within the height and width of the largest bubble. Print out the letter and full stop and cut them out. Lay the letter on the paper pattern for the bubble, and draw around it, then shift it slightly to the right and draw around it again. Repeat with the full-stop shape: draw around it once, then move it slightly to the right and draw around it again.

4 Cut the overlapped letter and full-stop shapes out of the bubble template.

5 Print out the letter and full stop twice more and cut them out.

1.

3.

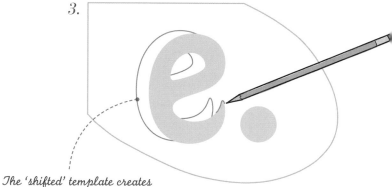

The 'shifted' template creates the shadow for the character on the finished bag.

5.

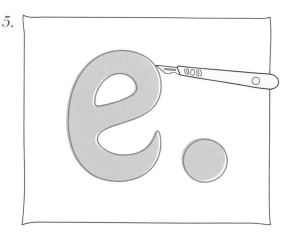

6 Using the brown-paper pattern for the bag and a ballpoint pen, draw around the back-and-front-flap piece, the front piece, the underflap piece and the side piece on the black leather and cut them out. Cut a second front piece out of the yellow leatherette.

7 Cut the three bubble shapes out of white leatherette (don't cut out the letter or the full stop). Cut one letter and full-stop pair out of black leatherette and a second out of grey leatherette.

8 Lay the bubble stencil over the largest white leatherette bubble and use a pencil to draw around the outline of the letter, the full stop and their overlapping shadows.

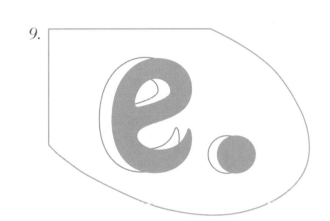

9 Using the hi-tack craft glue, stick the grey leatherette letter and full stop on to the right-hand outline of the pencil shape on the white leatherette.

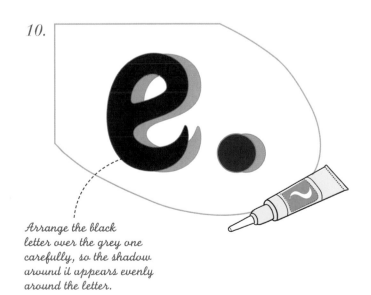

10 Stick the black leatherette letter and full stop on to the left-hand outline of the pencil shape on the white leatherette, so that it overlaps with the grey shape (which forms its 'shadow'), using hi-tack craft glue. Leave to dry.

Arrange the black letter over the grey one carefully, so the shadow around it appears evenly around the letter.

11 Spread the hi-tack craft glue on the back of all three leatherette bubbles and stick them in place on the yellow leatherette flap piece. Leave to dry.

12 When the glue is dry, stab stitch around the edges of the grey and black letters, the full stop, and around the edges of all three bubbles, using matching threads, a sturdy needle and a thimble.

13 Lay the yellow front piece on a flat surface. Take the back-and-front-flap piece of black leather and spread a thin line of hi-tack craft glue around the inside edge of half the window. Carefully position the glued edge over the yellow front piece so that it is aligned within the window and stick it down. Now repeat for the second half of the window.

14 Using black thread and a leather needle in your sewing machine, sew around the frame on the flap, just inside the edge of the leather, reverse stitching at the start and finish of the seam to secure it. Trim off the excess yellow leatherette on the back of the flap.

12.

13.

The window is easier to stick to the front piece if it's glued in two halves, top first, then bottom, as shown.

14.

15 Cut two lengths of webbing, each 15 cm (6 in.) long. Thread 5 cm (2 in.) of each length through a plastic loop and pin that end 5 cm (2 in.) below the other end of the webbing. Stitch a line across the webbing near the loop, reverse stitching at the start and finish to secure.

16 Turn in the raw edges of the webbing and pin them in place.

17 Take the piece of leather that will form the sides of the bag and stitch the webbing loops in place 2.5 cm (1 in.) from either end, centred on the width. Place the raw edges against the leather, neat side out, and box stitch around the edges of the webbing pieces, as shown, for extra strength.

18 Pull the strip of hook-and-loop tape apart, and machine stitch the loop side on to the front of the black leather underflap of the bag, 2.5 cm (1 in.) from the curved edge and centred on the width. Sew the hook side of the tape on to the front of the black leather front piece, 6 cm (2½ in.) from the curved bottom edge and centred on the width.

15.

17.

18.

Make sure the hoop-and-loop tape pieces are laid absolutely flat before they are sewn.

19 Using the contact adhesive and spatula, spread a thin line of adhesive along the edges on the wrong side of the window end of the back-and-front-flap piece and the black underflap piece. Leave both pieces to dry for a few minutes, then align them carefully, wrong sides together, and press firmly together to stick securely.

20 Machine stitch around the outside edge of the window in the front flap, 2 mm (¹⁄₁₆ in.) in from the edge.

21 Fold the strip for the sides of the bag in half and mark the centre point on both edges on the back of the strip, using a ballpoint pen. Fold the bag's front piece in half, right sides together, and mark the centre point of the bottom edge. Repeat on the back-and-front-flap piece, on the other end from the window.

22 Using the contact adhesive and spatula, spread a thin line of adhesive around the side and bottom edges of the front of the bag on the reverse side, and another line all along one side of the strip for the sides. Leave the glue to dry for a minute, then align the side piece all along the edges of the front, matching the centre marks together, and press firmly together to secure.

23 Machine stitch a line 5 mm (³⁄₁₆ in.) along the side/front pieces where they have just been glued together.

19.

21.

22.

When the strip is firmly glued in place, it forms the gusset for the bag.

24 Repeat steps 22 and 23 to attach the back-and-front-flap piece of the bag to the side strip, first gluing and then stitching the seam.

25 Use hi-tack craft glue to stick the upper edge of the underflap and the front of the bag together. Press firmly and leave to dry.

26 Take a piece of webbing 139 cm (55 in.) long and stitch a 115-cm (45-in.) length of reflective tape on to it, leaving a 15-cm (6-in.) length of webbing at one end uncovered, and using yellow thread.

27 Thread the plastic buckle on to the 15-cm (6-in.) length of webbing free at one end of the strap. Fold the raw end in and pin it down to the strap 2.5 cm (1 in.) from the end of the reflective tape, then machine stitch across the strap to secure.

28 Thread the loose (buckle-free) end of the strap through one of the plastic loops on the bag, with the reflective tape facing inwards, and then back up through the buckle and through the loop on the other side of the bag. Fold in the raw edge of the webbing and stitch it down.

25.

26.

Press the reflective tape as flat as possible with your fingers as you sew — it has a tendency to ruck up.

27.

Templates

{BABY} BLOCKS
Shown actual size.

{ONE-LETTER} DOORSTOP
Shown at 25%; enlarge by 400% for actual size.

TOP (CUT 1)

BASE (CUT 1)

FRONT/BACK (CUT 2)

SIDE (CUT 2)

{AMPERSAND} BOOKENDS

Shown at 50%; enlarge
by 200% for actual size.

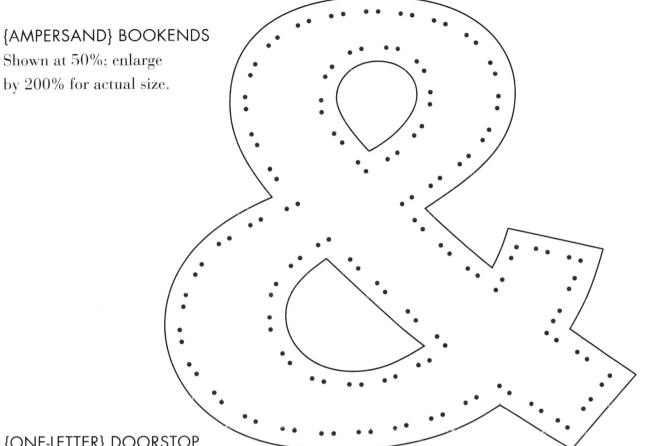

{ONE-LETTER} DOORSTOP

Shown at 25%; enlarge
by 400% for actual size.

SIDE (CUT 2)   TOP/BOTTOM (CUT 2)   FRONT/BACK (CUT 2)

{SHINY-LETTER}
WASHBAG
Shown at 70%;
enlarge by 143%
for actual size.

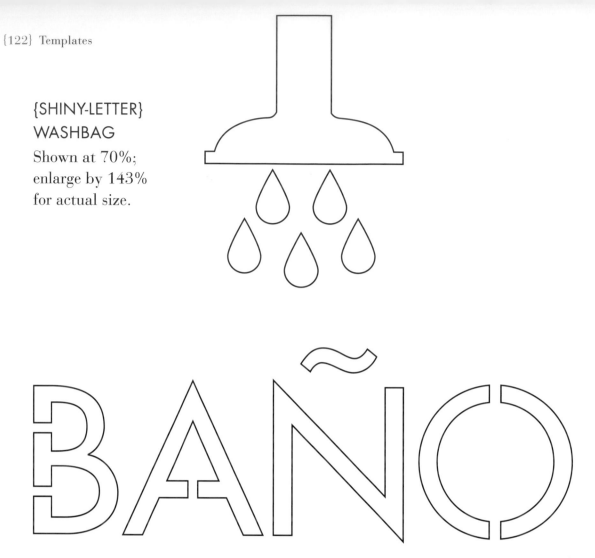

{LETTERED} CUSHIONS

Shown at 25%; enlarge by 400% for actual size.

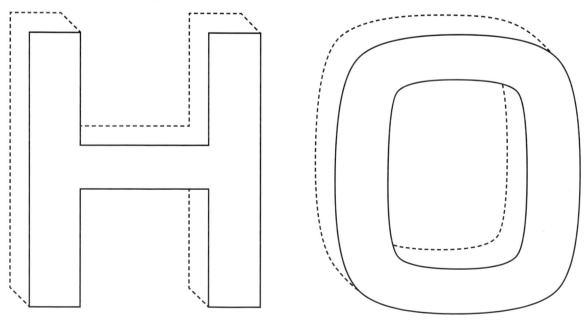

{LANGUAGE} POT HOLDERS

Shown at 70%; enlarge by 143% for actual size.

{CHEF'S} APRON

Shown at 70%;
enlarge by 143%
for actual size.

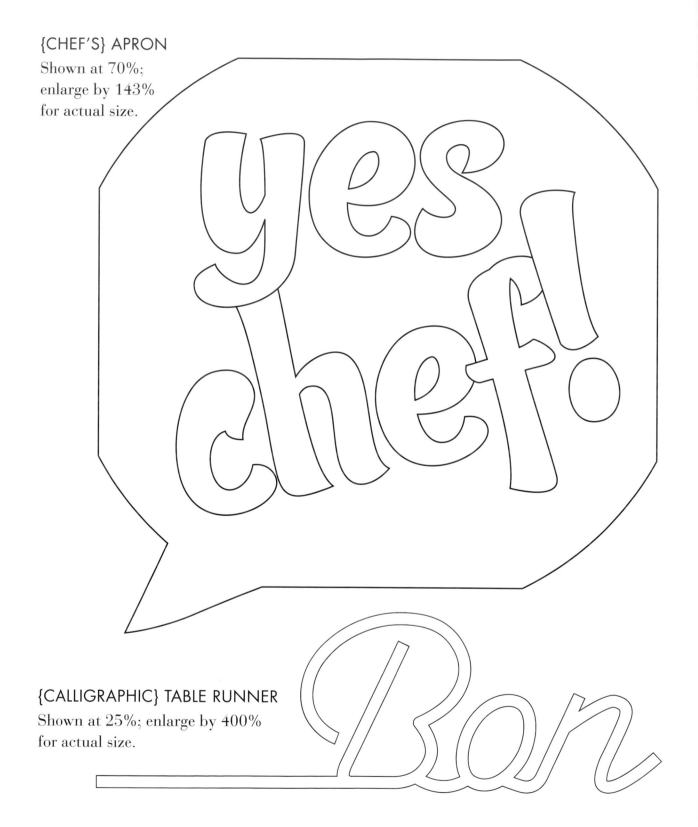

{CALLIGRAPHIC} TABLE RUNNER

Shown at 25%; enlarge by 400%
for actual size.

{CAFÉ} BLIND

Shown at 25%;
enlarge by 400%
for actual size.

{TABLET} CASE

Enlarge to match the size of your tablet.

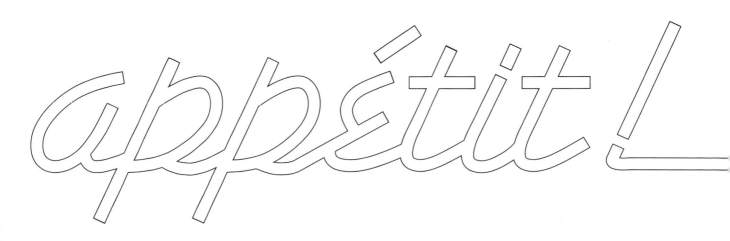

{INITIALLED} MESSENGER BAG

Shown at 25%; enlarge by 400% for actual size.

FLAP

FRONT OF BAG

BUBBLE SHAPE AND LETTER

SIDE OF BAG

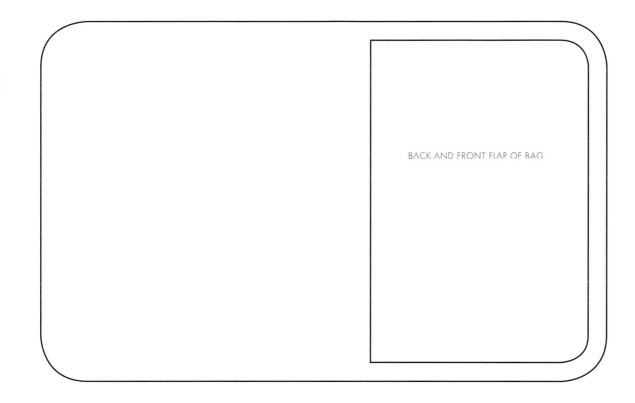

BACK AND FRONT FLAP OF BAG

{GARLAND} BUNTING

Shown at 25%; enlarge by 400% for actual size.

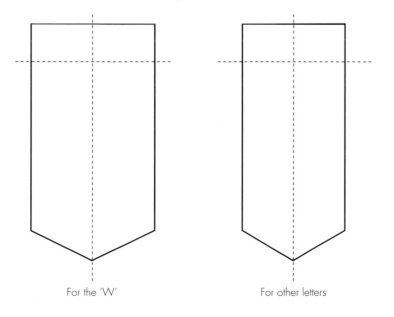

For the 'W'   For other letters

Index